Awake

&

Aware

Top Priority: Self

by
Cathy LaCounte

To Mother Earth.
Thank you so much for your unconditional love and for your patience as we play out our human drama on our way to a higher frequency. I feel privileged to be here with you, working with you, as we make this shift. Love you.

Table of Contents

Acknowledgements

Thanks to Laura Martinson for her proofreading help and her general support every day as my dear friend.

Thanks to Jimm Nawrocki for his beautiful cover art.

Thanks to all my teachers, fellow lightworkers and experiencers through the years. There are too many of you to mention. Thank you all for your courage and endurance.

Introduction

The first part of this book is mundane level things that, even if you don't totally agree with me on all counts, you'll probably at least relate at some level, as you too observe the symptoms of a very dysfunctional human society here on planet Earth.

The next part is mostly about influences in our lives that you may not be aware of. Our lives have been influenced in a disempowering way for generations, for millennia. All facets of our lives have been part of this influencing, be it religion, science, education, government and politics, media, commerce, big business, banking, our food and water supplies, modern medicine, the alteration of history, you name it. Many people talk about the world's problems, not realizing that what they are really seeing are not the original issues, but symptoms of them. The causes are still hidden from most people. Issues we see at a personal level can often be not as unique and personal as we might first think. We share the same issues and dysfunctions with our fellow humans, as we are all living in the same world environment. We often blindly donate to the problems of the world as unwitting pawns. These things could not go on without our participation and yet people continue to play a role because they have no idea how the whole global agenda is implemented. "Forgive them Father, they know not what they do."

There are cosmic energetic cycles also at work here. Some of those cycles last thousands of years. Just as sure as there is night and day, there are also much longer eras of oscillations affecting our planet and solar system. There are Golden Ages of enlightenment and Dark Ages of being isolated or shielded from enlightening cosmic energies. Combine a Dark Age with a time of heavy control by those in power and you end up in a very disempowered state, indeed.

Throughout, I address how our bodies really work, as opposed to what we've been conditioned to believe. I also discuss how our bodies have much to communicate to us if we would only learn the language that they speak, and listen. Our emotions too have much to tell us. We must learn to not stuff those emotions so we can gain from their wisdom.

The times we are presently in are a time of change, a time of chaos. Dual meaning of Chaos - Crisis or Opportunity. Which do we choose?

I so hope that your reading of this book is only the start or another step in the study of such topics. Some topics I just touch on briefly, just to help you think about how these areas of our lives are playing their role in keeping us disempowered. I've provided names, books and websites throughout, and not just buried in the bibliography, so that you can further investigate the topics that pique your interest. I don't care to reinvent the wheel and the folks I've referenced do a very good job at expressing the details of their particular area of research / wisdom. I'll do my best to present a large part of the big picture, but, if you want more details, go to the work of those folks referenced.

Everything presented here is an opinion or a perspective, whether it's mine or someone else's. That's all anyone has to offer. Please don't swallow all of this hook, line and sinker, without question, without further investigation. Engage your own discernment skills with this or ANY material. Be your own expert, your own authority, your own test for your own truth. I'm hoping to inspire self-empowerment in everyone who reads this. Please be a heretic, which literally means "one who thinks for oneself."

Our lives are multifaceted, so are our wounds and dysfunctions and so is our healing. I'm hoping here to bring enough of this wisdom together in one place to give the big picture on how we have gotten to this place and to demonstrate how we can re-prioritize our lives to better serve ourselves, others, and the world. Bear with me, as the big picture of this human earthly drama is very big, indeed. As I've said, if these perspectives are new to you, I would hope that you pay attention to what piques your interest and look up the books, videos and websites I've referenced and continue on your quest, and consult with one or both of the big G's - God or Google.

I hope this book will be of great assistance in your personal transformation. There is a great awakening occurring. If you're not already on board, I hope you will join us.

In times of change, learners inherit the earth, while the learned find themselves beautifully equipped to deal with a world that no longer exists. - Eric Hoffer.

Awake & Aware -Top Priority: Self

Awake & Aware

Top Priority: Self

THE COMMONALITY OF ALL IN EXISTENCE IS VIBRATION

There's the concept that, in the beginning, God spoke the word. This can, of course, have different meaning for each person who reads or hears it. To me, it means God spoke the word, the word was sound, the sound was vibration, and all of existence was set into motion.

Vibration is what all of existence has in common, be it matter, light, sound, magnetism, electricity, emotion, thought, color, smell, etc. As above, so below. Electrons circle - cycle, oscillate, vibrate, revolve - around an atom's nucleus. Moons circle planets, planets circle stars, stars circle galaxies. Everything vibrates. Everything has a frequency of rotation, revolution or vibration.

Toss a rock in a pond. A wave radiates outward. Toss another rock in and another wave radiates outward. Where those two waves meet, yet another wave is produced. The vibration of one thing affects the vibration of another.

Scientists go deeper and deeper into matter only to find through quantum physics that eventually they cannot detect with their five senses or amplification of their senses anything that could still be considered "matter," and yet there is still energy that cannot be perceived with our five senses which then affects the perceivable particles. I often ask folks, "What does the 'e' in e-mail stand for?" The answer: "Electronic". Next question, "What does the 'e' in e-motion stand for?" The answer: "Electron". E-motion = electron motion. Our e-motions are energies that affect the physical world of matter. The beginning of creation is energy. It all starts there. When dealing with re-pairing anything in our physical world, don't we find it's best to get down to the nitty gritty of things, to find the source of the problem, to nip it in the bud? Then, when we can, why not address the energetic level FIRST since it is what is ultimately affecting our physical world?

Furthermore, we are all connected, all part of the whole. Our "separateness" is merely an illusion. Michael Talbot, in his book *The Holographic Universe*, discusses the work of physicist, David Bohm, and neurophysiologist, Karl Pribram. The Universe itself is a projection, a hologram, the whole in every part. Everything interpenetrates everything.

What we perceive as the solidity of our physical world is actually a blur of frequencies. As an analogy, the only place a television signal is visible is on our TV screen. Everywhere else that signal exists, as it travels from the broadcast station, through the air, through the circuitry of our TVs, it is just an unseen frequency, a vibration. For a great article about Talbot's Holographic Universe, go to www.crystalinks.com/holographic.html

Our language has so much to reveal to us. If we look at the word origins, "individual" and "indivisible" come from the same root. We are always connected. The energy we have the most influence over though is our own. And like the wave in the pond, our energy radiates outward to affect other people and all life on this planet and the Cosmos. It all starts with self.

CENTERED ON SELF

Self-centered.

What comes to mind for you when you hear that term? Is it a whole string of so-called "negative" associations? Do you think selfish, inconsiderate, greedy, mean, aloof, uncaring, self-absorbed?

This term, like so much of our language, has been so corrupted, twisted and demonized. So many of our words and terms have lost their true meaning, their true vibration. I often call myself a word worker. I am constantly increasing my awareness of words' true vibration. These days, I look up all kinds of words in dictionaries. It doesn't matter if I think I already know the definition. I want to trace etymology and word origin. I want to know the TRUE VIBRATION of a word. The way we think and live has been so very tainted by this corruption of our language. Words and our feelings about them are very powerful. Over time, we have turned positive, empowering terms into something evil. And along with the words and terms, we turn positive, empowering ways of being into something evil also. The end result is we often don't do those positive empowering things because we have demonized them. I guess when we get to the point of turning everything positive and empowering in this world into something evil then we'll have a world full of evil - at least in our

4

own self-made reality. Everywhere we look we will see nothing but evil. What kind of a world is that to live in? Not some place I care to be. How 'bout you?

The energetic level, although the most subtle, is also the most significant. The energy we all generate inwardly and radiate outwardly affects the world far more than anything we could "do" in this world. Furthermore, the intentional energy behind our "doing" is the most powerful part of that doing. Have you ever noticed that if you go for a walk when you are in a really good mood, all happy and content, you get a whole lot of people smiling and saying hello? What did you "do" for those people? You did not "do" anything. Just you "being" happy made them happy. It was contagious and it was something they wanted to "catch". They "reached out" to embrace, to receive your happy mood and smiles with their own smiles and greetings. And when you are in a grumpy, irritable, exhausted state of mind and emotion and go out into the world, people tend to not smile or say hello or perhaps even make eye contact with you. They sense that downer, cloud-over-your-head energy and want no part of it. Who could blame them? By doing their best to not acknowledge you in your cloudy mood, to not connect with you, they are subtly protecting themselves, shielding themselves from your energy.

Just little, simple everyday experiences like these demonstrate how people around us are affected by our moods, our energy. The whole world, the universe, the entirety of existence is affected by our energy. Are you sure you are radiating out to existence the energy you want to? If you could visibly see that energy as something representative of how it feels, would you rather be filled with and radiating sunshine or pollution?

All dis-ease starts at the energetic level. Ease or the lack thereof is not a tangible, material thing, and yet dis-ease is an example of how that lack of ease is manifesting at the physical level. Our mental and emotional energy will manifest our health or dis-ease in our physical body.

Our energy also affects the world around us. Our world, our reality reflects back to us our inner energy. I used to own a brewery and I had T-shirts made up that played with the word "beer," which can be split into be-er, someone who is "being". The shirts said,

"Be-er Be what you want the world to be." Don't you want the world to be happy? Then be happy.

> *Make yourself so happy, that when others look at you they become happy too. - Yogi Tea Bag Tab Wisdom (wisdom is where you find it)*

Now if more folks would only help the world by helping themselves first, we could turn this whole thing around. Worry is focused energy, a prayer for something you don't want. Don't worry. Be happy.

Someone related this story to me. At an enlightenment conference a couple decades ago, the speaker was talking about taking care of your own needs and desires first, tending to your own self-nurturing and self-healing. A woman stood up and she was so very angry that it was not only detectable in her words and tone, but also in her body, which was tensed and stiff. She let the speaker know just how very upset she was with him that he would dare to encourage people to address their own lives first when there was so much pain and suffering and problems in the world. Another woman asked the angry woman if all the world's problems went away what she would be doing. She said she would be dancing. As she told of all the joy that dancing brought to her life, the energy she radiated very obviously shifted. She was no longer tense and stiff, but instead she exuded sheer joy and bliss. I think I'd personally rather hang out with the latter version of this woman than the former.

Joanie Vogel (www.energysinger.com/forecast.html) puts out a daily forecast on her website. One of her messages is:

> *You are the cup. It is your responsibility to fill up your own cup. You do not drink from someone else's cup. You do not let others drink from your cup. You fill up your cup by giving time to yourself every day. You establish and maintain a healthy relationship with your Creator daily. Daily meditation and contemplation fill up your cup. Regular self-care. Eventually, after time, you are giving and receiving daily, the blessings of spiritual well being. "Your cup runneth over." (and continues to do so, because you continue to give to your self.) Eventually, the constant continual inflow, creates OVERFLOW, causing your cup to 'runneth over'. (You didn't think it was real did you?) It is*

this overflow that you gift to the world at your choosing.
This overflow is pure unconditional love in its highest
vibration. The supply is endless. There are no strings
attached to your giving. You have found your self and
given generously. You love your self. YOU ARE THE
CUP!

Let your cup runneth over. The phrase "I am" can be finished
with "that". "I am that". We are all connected and everything you
see is part of yourself. There is most certainly everything right
about loving others, but let's get our priorities straight. Love thyself
first. Your cup can't runneth over until it's filled itself.

Byron Katie, in her book *I Need Your Love: Is That True?*, said
that she'd never been much of a spiritual person, but has always
lived by "love thy neighbor as thyself." Unfortunately, she didn't use
to love herself. This is where so very much of what we term "the
world's problems" comes from. It's from a lack of those things that
start with self. Self-love, self-respect, self-nurturing, self-
centeredness. How can we expect to love our neighbors when we
can't even love ourselves?!

Self centered. Where else to be centered but on self? Should
we be centered somewhere "over there?" Sadly enough, many,
many people are centering themselves somewhere "over there."
Their lives circle around someone else. Have you noticed that more
and more as of late, the charities that get the most publicity are
those that are dealing with people and issues on the other side of
the world? Even celebrities and Joe Averages who want to adopt
children are adopting children from foreign countries, as if there are
no children to adopt in their own country, their own back yard. I told
this to someone who then said that Mother Teresa said Americans
need not concern themselves with the issues in other parts of the
world, as there is plenty for them to work on in their own country.
Kind of begs the question - are people in Japan, China, Africa,
Europe, South America being encouraged to help stop poverty in
America? If we all took care of what was right in front of us,
wouldn't it all get taken care of?

Don't get me wrong, if you are moved to adopt a child from
another country or your inner voice tells you to donate to some
charity, by all means listen to your heart. What I am communicating

here is that there is an agenda set in the higher levels of control in this world to move your focus as far away from yourself, your own healing and your own back yard as possible. The further you are from your center, the less power you have. I'm just asking you to be aware of this agenda and to take your power back. Wouldn't our own back yard be a better place to start than the other side of the world? And those that we helped would then help others and it would spread across our globe until everyone was taken care of. The place to start is not "over there," but "in here".

> *"Truly the greatest gift you can give is that of your own self-transformation."*
> *- Lao Tzu*

How can our own personal growth, healing and transformation ever take place if our focus is always somewhere "out there?"

DEMONIZATION OF POWER

There are many ways in this realm to tap into our power and connect with both Spirit and Earth. The entities here that have dared to try to control us know of these. Through many generations, through the millennia, since our beginnings, "they" have attempted to keep us down, to disempower us. Their methods have been many, not the least of which being messing with our psyches. We've been subjected to a barrage of propaganda and brainwashing since the get-go. After all of this going on for as long as it has, many of us at this point are in a place where we can't imagine anything beyond our brainwashed paradigm. We've been conditioned to believe that the very things that would empower us are evil. Those things that ARE our power have become demonized.

Demonization of Hell, the Underworld or the Lake of Fire

Yep, you heard that right. Hell has been demonized. "Of course", you say. Nope. There's no "of course" to it. Going through our own personal Hell is the very thing that enables us to face our own demons, to heal our wounds, to return to our true selves, to regain the power that is rightfully ours, to become the gods and goddesses that we truly are. Many ancient texts refer to crossing the Lake of Fire. The alchemists spoke of turning lead into gold,

8

which is more symbolic than literal. It's about turning a mortal, mundane human back into a god. As the alchemists' symbology teaches us, it is the "fire" of life experience that creates the catalyst for healing. Alchemy uses the metaphor of heating metal. When metal is heated, the dross, the impurities rise to the surface so that they may be skimmed off, leaving only the pure metal. The same is true for our issues, our wounds, which the "fire" of our Hellish experiences allows to surface. The Lake of Fire, Hell, allows our emotional and psychological wounds to surface so that we may clear and release them, leaving only our true essence, which is wonderful, indeed.

And yet, we have been conditioned to do everything possible to avoid Hell. In our efforts to avoid Hell, all we are doing is pitching a tent there. The road to Heaven goes through Hell. And when going through Hell, it's best to keep going. Trying to avoid Hell is just what is causing us to camp out there. Be brave enough to face your wounds, your demons, in order to heal. Our literal and metaphoric conditioning has led us to want to avoid facing our wounds and fears head on. We get into all manner of addiction and avoidance to escape or put off facing our wounds.

The single biggest addiction in the world is busyness. Someone may say, "I don't do drugs or smoke and don't ever touch a drop of alcohol" and yet these folks may be indulging in one of the most common forms of escape there is. Maybe they are workaholics. Maybe it's that and / or activities, events, or whatever they can dream up to be focused "out there" instead of working on "in here." They keep their schedules very busy. They may not even like their jobs or the activities they do or maybe are frustrated beyond all recognition with the people they are around but will not stop since all that drama and dysfunction serves as such a wonderful distraction to keep them from addressing their own wounds and healing. Perhaps they have a messiah complex. They hang with people who have even more issues than they do so they can focus on the other person's issues rather than address their own.

Even spirituality is used as an escape. All that escapism suffices to do is build up pressure. But, the more pressure, the more likely something will eventually give way. Life is rather insistent that we get around to healing. The more we procrastinate, the larger and more in our faces our issues become. But this makes them easier to see. It gets more uncomfortable, but that's the whole point. Life wants us to be uncomfortable enough to actually knuckle down and make some changes, to move.

I watched an interview on CMN - Conscious Media Network. (www.consciousmedianetwork.com). The interview was with Phillip Mountrose on Emotional Freedom Technique. EFT can be used for healing by saying affirmations while tapping on accupressure meridian points. The affirmations have to do with the irritation or whatever that is bothering you. For example, he used this one, "Even though I am irritated that my boyfriend is not environmentally sensitive, I still love and accept myself." The interviewer, Regina Meredith, asked him about some folks thinking that this is improper use of affirmations, the common belief being that you don't affirm how things are, but how they will be when healed. Phillip said it takes both. You can't just talk about what bothers you then stop, just holding that, but you also can't ignore it. Phillip gave a great analogy. He said if you were going to remodel a room, you wouldn't put in all the nice new stuff and leave all the old junk in there. You want to clean out that junk. He acknowledged that the New Agers often don't understand that. Indeed. And with that, now some New Agers are just putting a new face on an old conditioned state that didn't work to empower us under any religious name.

Michael Tsarion (www.michaeltsarion.com) speaks of psychic hygiene. We're so obsessed with cleaning everything, our bodies, cars, houses, but we don't clean out our psyches. Take out the garbage regularly. You don't want that mental, emotional garbage piling up any more than you'd want the garbage to pile up in your kitchen. It too gets rather stinky after a while. Be courageous enough to make regular, voluntary Underworld visits. You will become "en-lightened," as in your load will be lightened. Why carry around all that old, unnecessary baggage? Face it and then let it go.

In helping others heal, I am very to the point, no nonsense. I often literally feel like an exorcist, and you can bet those old "demons" that people have stuffed so want to lash out at me. Never mind that the person would be happier, more at peace to let all that old emotional and psychological energy surface and release it. We co-created this realm to have experiences that are outside of Heaven, God's realm, the realm of the absolute. If we didn't want

10

these experiences, we wouldn't be here. These so-called "negative" experiences are EXACTLY why we came here. And we just camp out in our own self-made Hell by not being brave enough to just face the experience and move through it.

Here, again, we have been conditioned to think that some emoting is "bad". Body and mind have a close connection. Our thinking affects our physicality. Emotions and spirit have a close connection. It is a gift to this world to be sensitive, to be emotional. If we disconnect from emotion, we disconnect from spirit. Emotion has much to tell us, but we won't benefit from it if we judge it as bad and avoid or stuff it.

We don't let the emotional energy show itself, and henceforth, get stuck with it and it burbles up underneath and occasionally comes up to shoot bullets at whoever happens to be close by. It wants to come out. The only "bad" emotions are those that are not expressed. It wants to heal, to clear, to be released. But we're conditioned to not go to the Underworld, to not go into Hell, to not cross that Lake of Fire, and yet it's Heaven itself that awaits on the other side. The establishment absolutely knows this. They keep us from Heaven by convincing us to not go to Hell.

The next time someone tells ya to "go to Hell," you can tell 'em you think that's mighty fine advice. Race ya to the other side!

Demonization of Our Bodies

Yep, the more we procrastinate, the larger and more in-our-faces our issues become. That makes for a nice segue into another powerful thing that has been demonized - our bodies. When we allow our emotional and psychological wounds to build up and we keep stuffing them down, eventually we will manifest that energy onto the physical level as chronic illness. There's a book by The Heyeokah Guru that I had to buy just for its subtitle. It's called *Adam and Evil – The God Who Hates Sex, Women and Human Bodies*. This book tells of how the Bible has been used to demonize all these powerful things.

Our bodies are on loan to us from Mommy Earth. Our bodies have much to communicate to us. Louise Hay has a book called *Heal Your Body* which tells the mental / emotional energy behind all bodily afflictions, be it dis-ease, injury or accidents, for there are no

11

accidents in life. Things happen for a reason. Our bodies are an expression of our personality energy. If we allow our wounds to burble under long enough without addressing them, our bodies will express to us what needs to be worked on through injury, accident or chronic illness / dis-ease. And here our bodies have been demonized and we are taught not to listen to what our bodies are telling us. Get Louise's book for a quick reference to what your body is communicating to you, whether it's through a bruise, a strain, sprain, broken bones, dis-ease, discomfort, etc. The intensity of our affliction is directly related to the level of our resistance to our body's or Life's messages. Pain is caused by resistance to healing!

Demonization of Mistakes

A good friend of mine has a major beef with this. He can't stand that kids are pushed to perfection all the time. They're made to think that mistakes are a horrible thing. Mistakes are one of the best ways we have to learn. You can learn things a whole lot of other ways, but by God, if you make a mistake, you don't often forget that lesson. This push for perfection can drive people to just flat stop doing much of anything, to stop experiencing much of anything for fear of making a mistake.

> *"The man who makes no mistakes does not usually make anything." - Edward Phelps*

We come to this earthly realm to have experiences. Often those experiences are of the sort that we can't accomplish in the non-physical realm between lives. Since we bothered to come here, we may as well be here and have some experiences - "mistakes" and all.

> *"Mistakes are part of the dues one pays for a full life." - Sophia Loren*

Demonization of Being Alone, Intuition, Introspection

I care so very much about my fellow human. What I desire most for all of us is to heal and grow. Sometimes the best thing we can do for each other is to be there, but sometimes the best thing we can do is to not be there. Leaving someone's life or having them leave yours can be the catalyst for the next stage of growth. Also some of the best opportunities I've had to heal and grow was when, no matter how much I thought I needed someone to talk to, Life thought it best that I spend some alone time, some introspection time, some Underworld time. In those moments, I could not reach friends on the phone. I'd e-mail them only to learn weeks later that they'd been on vacation. That gave me the opportunity to "keep (w)holy the Sabbath." Sabbath literally means "to sit within yourself," and that introspection time is just exactly what was called for. Perfect.

Speaking of introspection and alone time, I read a wonderful article online titled *Against School - How public education cripples our kids, and why,* by John Taylor Gatto. Gatto is a former New York State and New York City Teacher of the Year and the author of The Underground History of American Education. If you'd like to know what's really being "taught" in our education system, I strongly recommend you seek out this article. It demonstrates how the medium IS the message. So much rhetoric over curriculum, but that's not what's really being taught. Just like the magician waving one hand emphatically, "Look over here, look over here!" while the other hand is where there's really something going on.

Here's an excerpt from John's article:

> *Once you understand the logic behind modern schooling, its tricks and traps are fairly easy to avoid. School trains children to be employees and consumers; teach your own to be leaders and adventurers. School trains children to obey reflexively; teach your own to think critically and independently. Well-schooled kids have a low threshold for boredom; help your own to develop an inner life so that they'll never be bored. Urge them to take on the serious material, the grown-up material, in history, literature, philosophy, music, art, economics, theology - all the stuff schoolteachers know well enough to avoid. Challenge your kids with plenty of solitude so that they can learn to enjoy their own company, to conduct inner dialogs. Well-schooled people are conditioned to dread being alone, and they seek constant companionship through the TV, the computer, the cell phone, and through shallow friendships quickly acquired and quickly abandoned. Your children should have a more meaningful life, and they can.*

Reminds me of a quote by Mark Twain, "Soap and education are not as sudden as a massacre, but they are more deadly in the long run."

Like I said, our alone time offers us some of the most productive healing and growth time we could have and yet we're conditioned to never be alone, to never look inside. Our most direct connection to God / Source / the Isness / the Divine / the One, whatever term you care to put to it, is inside.

You can look to the stars in search of the answers,
Look for God and life on distant planets
Have your faith in the ever after
While each of us holds inside the map to the labyrinth
And heaven's here on earth

Lyrics from "Heaven's Here on Earth" by Tracy Chapman

And then there's the old Chinese story about God and the devil having a conversation. God said, "Humans are always asking and praying and petitioning me for something. There are times that I'd just like to go hide behind the furthest star." The devil said, "You don't have to do that. You can just hide right behind their eyes. They'll never look there."

In esoteric symbology, there is the "Lions' Gate". The lions guard the gate. There's two ways to look at that. The lions are there to help you through or to keep you from going through the gate. The gate, like William Henry speaks of, may be a stargate, which is the door to a wormhole that not only can transport us through time and across distance, but also connects us to other dimensions and to our "higher self", the aspect of ourselves that perhaps "resides" at the galactic core of our Milky Way galaxy. Some would say the ego is the lion at the gate that keeps us from connecting to our higher selves. Some would say that religion itself has, instead of showing us the way, actually kept us from it. The ego is not all bad, just overused and misused due to conditioning. And those people who truly are on a personal quest and are honing their discernment skills can glean much information from the teachings of many and perhaps all religions.

The "God(s)" of the Old Testament are not who we've been led to believe, but instead are entities posing as gods. In convincing humanity they were the one true God, they have, in essence, disconnected us from the one true God. William Henry (www.williamhenry.net) had this to say in his book *The Healing Sun Code*:

> *From this point forward in the Old Testament, humanity was taught not to look within to our spiritual nature, for to do so is "bad". Furthermore, E.A. and the Skilled teachers of other ancient traditions and teachings related to spiritual salvation, were so demonized that even today no average person would dare go near them for fear of being labeled a devil worshipper, a Satanist, or in the modern vernacular, a "New Ager". These Family Secrets are missing because the Church viewed the serpentsoul(s) who dwells in the Tree (Ark) and originally delivered them as a monster. We must remember that monsters symbolize the guardian of a treasure, immortality for example. I find it fascinating that the word monster is the same as minster or minister. As noted, Min is the root for minister, a conduit between man and God and Minne, the name given to Aphrodite, the Goddess of Love. Ministers guard the secret treasure within.*

Yes, serpentsoul. That takes us into the next thing...

Demonization of Serpent Energy

Michael Tsarion (and others) tells us that many ancient texts, not the least of which being the Druid texts, which are the world's oldest, tell a very different Garden of Eden story than the one we heard in Sunday school. About 50,000 years ago (depending on who's doing the interpreting), a race of visitors came to this planet. The visitors' leaders were two brothers, Enlil and Enki. These two account for the Old Testament schizophrenic love / fear "God." What was documented in Sumerian texts, where the Old Testament was drawn from (amongst other ancient texts), is these two "gods" Enlil and Enki, not the one true God. That's why the original writings of the Old Testament spoke in plural "Let US make man in OUR image."

Long story, but about 14,000 years ago, they genetically engineered the first Adamic race from their own genes and those of a local hominid. This is what accounts for the so-called "missing link" or a grand "evolutionary" leap in intelligence in local hominids. It wasn't evolution at work, but genetic engineering. Since we're now dabbling in that ourselves these days, this is not such a long way to stretch our imaginations. If today's genetic engineers can create Franken Food, aka Genetically Modified Organisms (GMOs) or green glowing pigs (I kid you not, look it up) by splicing jelly fish genes into pigs, then I guess a highly advanced ancient race of beings could genetically design beings also, namely us.

The supposed intention of genetic engineer Enki was to create a slave race. That may have been a cover to keep his brother Enlil happy. I, and others, have reason to think that our original genetic engineer who created humans, Enki (or E.A.), was really attempting to repair a mistake that his race had made. They had created a solar system catastrophe that released many souls at once in a very traumatic state, which kept them trapped here in reincarnation cycles. His true reason for creating a new race may have been to create a soul resurrection machine called the human being / modern man / homo sapien, that could be used to free these trapped souls.

Enki's original creation was a very intelligent race that was just too smart to go for that slave stuff. They rebelled and moved to another continent called Lemuria or Mu. The visitors were back at it and created a second Adamic race. They dumbed down this second race. In my mind, this is where the polarized, dualistic nature of things took hold in a big way, where the genders were split and the human brain split into hemispheres. The "serpent" in the garden was really the first highly intelligent Adamic race, the Lemurians. They told the second Adams and Eves that the visitors tried to turn themselves into slaves and the second Adamic race was their next attempt. They told of their own rebellion and let the Adams and Eves know they did not have to be slaves either. So that "nasty serpent" didn't want a new race of people (us) to be slaves and for this has been demonized for millennia. The ones doing the demonizing were Enlil and gang, who were control freaks who wanted to enslave the human race. Their influence continues to this day. This second rebellion resulted in the war between Atlantis (the visitors) and Lemuria (Mu), where the first Adamic race made home.

William Henry speaks of references, of many ancient cultures, to serpent or dragon energies. The wavy line made by a serpent's movement can be very representative of electro-magnetic energy, a standing wave, cosmic rays. Much information is coming out about how the symbology surrounding messiah characters like Jesus, and so very many others that share that same symbology, has to do with the zodiac and sun worship. Our own sun being a symbol of many other "suns" both inward and outward - our own inner suns and the galactic core. As above, so below. Microcosms and macrocosms. Knowledge of how to tap into this serpent energy will allow us to be the soul resurrection machines and gods that we were designed to be. Freedom, sweet freedom.

Serpent energy is also often associated with Kundalini energy traveling up and down our spines, through our seven main chakras, which then brings us to the next "demon."

Demonization of Sex

Sex has most certainly been demonized and, due to that, we've gotten to the point where many people are scared to talk about it, to learn about it and to teach about it. By making it taboo, we've dirtied it all up. Sexually wounded people pass on their wounds "in secret" through rape, molestation or even through the "ee gad" reaction when children do what comes naturally and explore their own and each other's bodies. There is nothing inherently evil in this world, it all depends on the intent behind it. The establishment has certainly managed to mess up the whole intent of sex, to make many people feel dirty about sex, to make profane something that is very sacred. Sex is not just for pleasure or procreation, it's who we are.

Diane Stein, in her book *Essential Reiki,* speaks of the three energies that flow through us - Heavenly Ki (or chi), Earthly Ki and Original Ki. Original Ki is our own energy, it is our direct connection to spirit and it IS sexual energy. When someone does energy movement throughout their body using visualization / meditation techniques, it is sexual energy that they are working with. Diane speaks of initially tapping into the second chakra during these energy movement visualizations. The second chakra, which is an energy center a few inches below our belly buttons, is about sex, creativity (and procreation) and desire. You would start with that sexual energy, move it to the third or gut chakra at your solar plexus and put the fire of your internal sun behind it, your will power, then circulate it through your remaining chakras from there.

For an in-depth study of the chakra system, I highly recommend Anodea Judith's *Wheels of Life: A User's Guide to the Chakra System*. By healing, clearing and balancing our chakras, we can be a better antenna from Heaven to Earth to help bring Heaven to Earth or raise Earth to Heaven. Sex is a VERY big part of connecting Heaven to Earth, and yet religions have been used by the establishment to brainwash folks into thinking that the very thing that provides our strongest, most natural connection to Heaven is somehow evil. It is all part of the disempowering global control agenda.

Tom Kenyon and Judi Sion, in their book *The Magdalen Manuscript – The Alchemies of Horus & the Sex Magic of Isis*, tell of a visualization meditation that moves the two serpents, masculine and feminine energy, up through the chakras, which can produce an orgasm. As it is said, orgasm is something that happens in the brain, in the pineal gland to be exact. Sex is just our very natural way of connecting Heaven to Earth, of being an antenna to do so, of becoming the soul resurrection machines we were designed to be. Believe me, this visualization meditation technique absolutely works. :-) One significant thing brought out in this book is a practical use for the generated sexual energy. The ecstatic energy, whether generated through such meditative techniques or through sex, can be used to energize our Ka or light bodies. In so doing, we are preparing our Ka bodies for ascension. Our Ka bodies are "light" or perhaps another way to express it would be to say that they are higher frequency, lower density than our physical bodies, but they occupy the same space as our physical bodies and look the same. Mary Magdalen, through Tom and Judi, tells us of how she used her knowledge of sex magic to help Jesus prepare his light body for ascension after the crucifixion.

We're supposed to experience pleasure, of all sorts, not just sexual. As a matter of fact, our mind and body are meant to run on pleasure - move toward the pleasure and away from the pain. But I think the conditioning of thinking sex is somehow bad has bled over into other areas of our lives and we start to thinking that not only is sex bad, but all pleasure is evil in some way or can only come from things that are harmful or, at the very least, that pleasure is just some fleeting thing that we don't pay much attention to in between all our "busyness". We've been conditioned to replace real pleasure with addictions. With some substances, it would serve us to recognize the difference between use and ab-use. We even become addicted to pain and suffering, drama and playing the victim.

Learn to look for those happy times in life and to really get into them, no matter how simple. Don't worry, be happy. Enjoy your tea, your bath, your quiet time, the sun on your face, playing with your dog or your kids, learning and creating, doing nothing, whatever brings you happiness in that moment. Acknowledge these things and be grateful for them and your attitude of gratitude will bring you more of the good stuff. And that joyful, happy energy will be radiated out to a world that could use it as much as you do. I will take this opportunity to state again, that the energetic level is the most subtle, but the most significant, the most powerful. And, again, with that goes that same Yogi Tea Bag Tab wisdom I quoted earlier that says, "Make yourself so happy you make everyone around you happy."

One thing to be aware of is that there is a great energy exchange during sex. With this exchange comes the potential to take on our sex partner's issues. Presently, that's a good enough reason to not be promiscuous. But now that you know about this energy exchange, that in and of itself, that sheer awareness, will provide some protection. Setting your intent to not take on others' issues will help also. But, ultimately, trust your inner voice when you sense another's energy and perhaps you could stand to be more selective. Now, if we all addressed our issues, healed our wounds, capitalized on Life's growth opportunities, we would be in a world where having many sex partners would not be an issue. We could actually realize the "free love" ideal that the flower children of the 60's and 70's were shooting for. Now, if that ain't reason enough to work on your own personal healing, what is I ask you!? :-) Talk about Heaven here on Earth. That would be sheer Nirvana. ;-)

Demonization of the Occult

Here, again, is something that has great power. And as with everything else I'm listing in this section, the occult is something used by the "people" running this world. But for everyone else, "they" have managed to paint it as something black and evil. People have bought into that lie and since they don't want to do something evil they avoid tapping into the power of the occult. Some think that the true meaning of occult is "that which is hidden." Well, because many followers of the occult down through the ages were harassed or killed, it certainly did become hidden. But that is not the original vibration, the word origin of the word occult. Oc (or ak) means light. The occult is very literally the cult or culture of light. And, yes, for the last 13,000 years or so, we've certainly been in the dark side of the Great Year / Cycle, which has to do with the precession of the equinoxes and lasts approximately 26,000 years. Yes, the culture of light has most certainly become hidden. Let's bring it back, shall we.

The Holocaust offers an example of a world leader persecuting people for what they may have known. There is so much emotion concerning the Holocaust. The focus of such is often on Jews. This was not an atrocity just towards Jews, but towards humans. Period. By making the focus ONLY on Jews, this has served as a distraction away from what was really going on there. This has also served as a "divide and conquer" mechanism. It's very difficult for humans to see how they are all being abused when they keep looking at each other as the abusers. In order to have a deeper understanding of the overall agenda involved, one must look at ALL the groups persecuted by Hitler and the Nazis. They flat attempted to wipe out the Gypsies and today's "rulers" are still working on that. Some would say this is a major factor in the whole Bosnia / Serbia thing. Hitler outlawed freemasonry, Wiccan and pagan practices and other occult practices, such as astrology. If you start to look at what all these groups have in common, you'll get closer to the truth. Along with the Jews, these other groups had, to some degree or another, held onto ancient wisdom. Such wisdom is very powerful and allows us to tap into the true spiritual, god / Christ beings that we are. Hitler had his own astrologers and other occult advisors, so it wasn't that he thought these things were bad. Au contraire Mofrair. He knew the power in this information. When he got to the top, he wanted to pull the ladder up behind him. He could use these power tools but no one else could.

He even persecuted homosexuals. It's all for the same reasons - power. Like I said earlier, sex is VERY powerful and a very natural part of the human soul resurrection machines that we are. Homosexuals could tap into the power of sex without having to worry about the consequence of having children. Raising children can take time and effort away from being able to raise consciousness. I've known some folks who can and do pull off doing both, but it's not always an easy task, especially the way the world has been recently. I can't help but think those doing both are rather old souls and these days are raising very enlightened children. The potential of those children's enlightenment starts with the child themselves, such as with the Indigo Children and Crystal Children. For a good summary article on these children, go to www.starchild.co.za/what.html.

And the Aryans were Hitler's "chosen" people, but not for the reasons you might think. According to Arizona Wilder - see David Icke's interview with her called *Revelations of a Mother Goddess* - the Aryans are originally from Mars. Michael Tsarion and many others have also talked about this. Many times, I've asked people what the word indigenous means to them. I often get answers like Aboriginals, Africans, Native Americans. No one has yet to say white or Caucasian. It's like a part of us knows that the white race is not indigenous to this planet. The "people" running this world have literally used Aryans as energy sources. "They" (those running the world) are literal and energetic vampires and I'm sure if anyone of Aryan blood understood that they were actually the top menu selection, well, the Neo-Nazis might direct their energies towards some different things than what they have been up to. They just might direct their energies towards not letting the establishment feed on them instead of succumbing to divide and conquer and picking fights with the colored races.

One area of the occult is astrology. If astrology is such an "evil" thing in the Christian's world, then riddle me this, why is the zodiac the first thing you see when stepping into the Vatican? (See the movie *Zeitgeist* for some information about the zodiac in religious symbology. That won't be your stopping point on learning the significance of such things to all of us, but it's a good start.) If astrology and the science of astronomy are in conflict with religion, then why does the Vatican own and operate many of the big observatories around the world?

And religion and science seem to want to be at odds but they've much to share. One day, on TV, I caught a physicist speaking to some college students. He said his brother is very spiritual. The physicist and his cohorts may make some major "discovery." The physicist says he gets all excited and he calls his brother and tells him the details. His brother gives a ho hum response and says, "The Vedas have been saying that for millennia."

Some Christians are catching on to the global control agenda, but really only see the "left" side of the conspiracy. They don't see how religions have been used to disempower people. I've talked of how the occult is not a bad thing. There is nothing inherently good or evil in this world, it all depends on the Intent behind it. The Christians who are starting to understand the global control agenda, see how those in power are using the power of the occult for very negative, evil, abusive things but the Christians are still getting caught in thinking that the occult itself is bad. We all could stand to learn more about the occult and start using it for good, to take back the power that is rightfully ours. And we will do that not by harming others, but by just acknowledging and using our own power, letting our light shine. Like all those super hero stories where the question is posed, "Do you use your power for good or evil?" Those doing "evil" aren't scared to use these power tools. It's high time the rest of us who actually want to help this world and her inhabitants finally relearn the power in the occult and turn this whole thing around.

Demonization of Alchemy

How many times have you heard someone bring up alchemy and someone laughs about those wacky Middle Ages chemists who were trying to turn lead into gold. Ha, ha. This is not literal. It's symbolic. It's about turning mundane, simple humans into the god-men (which is what hu-man means) that we all truly are. I talked about some of this under the Demonization of Hell heading. Life's experiences, initiations, rites of passage serve to provide the catalyst for the opportunity to turn "lead" into "gold." Those who study the Mysteries of Life learn how to utilize these catalytic events to catapult themselves back to the Kingdom of Heaven. The prefix "cata" means "down." Ya gots to go down to go up. The road to Heaven goes through Hell. How many times do you hear of folks having a spiritual epiphany when they have hit rock bottom? It would serve us to flow with these Hellish challenges instead of fighting them. We only prolong our pain and suffering by trying to push off our Underworld visits.

Demonization of Lucifer

This leads us now into how Lucifer, the light bearer, has been demonized. For a good, concise history of the term Lucifer, see: www.lds-mormon.com/lucifer.shtml.

The term Lucifer was only used in the Bible once. It was in reference to a fallen Babylonian king, not a fallen angel or an "angel" of any sort. Lucifer is Latin for "light bearer / bringer." Latin, so, of course, that wouldn't be in an old Hebrew manuscript. In the Hebrew text, the expression used to describe the Babylonian king before his death is Helal, son of Shahar, which can best be translated as "Day star, son of the Dawn." (As the aforementioned article states, The name evokes the golden glitter of a proud king's dress and court much as his personal splendor earned for King Louis XIV of France the appellation, "The Sun King"). So when translated into Latin, yes, the term Lucifer meaning "light bearer" would be a good choice. Amazing that "the light bearer / bringer" morphed into the Prince of Darkness. Hilarious actually.

Lucifer is associated with the planet Venus, as it is the brightest thing in the sky past the Sun and Moon. More specifically, it is Venus when it is the Morning Star, low in the east in the morning. When Venus is the Evening Star, low in the west in the evening, it is called Vesper. Fundamentalist Christians could stand to note that the Bible has Jesus referencing himself as the morning star. I would guess that the concept of Jesus being a "fallen angel" wouldn't sit well in a fundamentalist Christian mind. The symbology, in this case, is more about an awakening of consciousness than anything else.

> *The planet Venus is the lightbringer, the first radiant beam that does away with the darkness of night. It is a symbol of the development of the divine light in man, for the first awakening of self-consciousness, for independent thinking and the real application of free will. It means the bringing of the light of compassionate understanding to the human mind. In this broader view the connection of the morning*

star with Jesus makes good sense, because compassion is the essence of Jesus' teaching.

From "Some Light on Lucifer" by Ina Beldris

The metaphor of Lucifer being applied to the Babylonian king had to do with him thinking he could rise above God. Little 'g' god perhaps? What "god" are we talking about here? A jealous one perhaps, not the One True God. This was word play to do with the fact that since Venus is in an inferior / lower orbit than Earth, we never see it traverse across the sky as the Sun and Moon do so it could not rise as high as those two orbs. The king could not rise as high as God / god.

So, somewhere over time, through translations, the idea of an evil fallen angel was concocted. I'm not sure that this was all that unintentional. Since Lucifer ultimately meant Venus as the Morning Star and Venus represents feminine energy, then perhaps those wanting to maintain the imbalance of the patriarchy may very well have been demonizing feminine energy.

The icon of "the devil" is also a conglomeration of feminine symbols and "connection" symbols put together. How 'bout them there horns. Michelangelo made his statue of Moses with horns. Some say this is a misinterpretation, but I can see it may be a very intentional use of the Language of the Birds (the Green Language). The horns represent the connection to spirit. According to the Wikipedia entry for Michelangelo's Moses:

> *The mistake in translation is possible because the word "keren" in the Hebrew language can mean either "radiated (light)" or "grew horns".*

Another interesting interpretation of these horns can be found online in the article called *Moses and Those 'Horns'* by Eloise Hart. An excerpt from that article:

> *Here possibly is where the idea of horns originates. For in the Mystery language horns are the sign of the successful neophyte, of one who has passed the dread tests of initiation and quite literally touched divinity.*

The red of the devil represents the bride or sexual feminine energy. (White would represent the pure youthful sister feminine

24

energy and blue would be the old wise woman feminine energy. Huh. Red, white and blue.) So, gee, two birds with one stone there – demonize women and sex by making "the devil" red. It's my understanding, decades ago, the Vatican admitted that "the devil" icon was of their own making. Not that that admission helps much to undo the damage done since this icon has become "common knowledge", never mind untrue common knowledge.

The corrupted use of the term Lucifer has most certainly, over time, become it's own entity in the collective conscious, a rather nasty entity, but a rather universal meme at this point. This situation reminds me of a sci-fi book I read years ago called Cirque. It was millennia in Earth's future and the city of Cirque sat on the edge of an abyss. The citizens dumped their garbage into the abyss, along with willing all their "sins" into it as well. After many years, something started to grow there and it was rather nasty. Our story reminds me of that novel because in our ignorant and veiled state we have dumped our crap onto an entity we've dreamed up named Lucifer. OUR crap. Nothing quite like shifting responsibility. And we've done it for so long that the story of that character has grown into something quite nasty. If there were any "fallen angels" here, it would be us, we Earth humans, stuck under a Sea of Glass as William Henry tells of. And just like a glass ceiling, this Sea of Glass is there but we can't see it and yet awareness of it plays a huge role in our ability to pass through it. We can regain that connection to spirit, grow our horns if you will, by becoming aware of that veil, that Sea of Glass.

In this discussion, I can't help but talk about angels in general. And interesting that Lucifer would be considered an angel. I've often wondered if angels are really entities or would it be more accurate to say they are *energies*. Then tying such symbols to math, are archangels the same as arc angles? Angels are supposedly here to serve human kind. Perhaps in our dense state of being we have such a tough time wrapping our minds and hearts around what angels are that we've collectively personified them as a way to tap into that energy. We can utilize that energy by calling on our personified image of them.

What's interesting for me concerning Lucifer is that the collective idea / creation of what Lucifer is never resonated with me. I understand the Hebrews never have considered there to be some "devil" type entity. I'd have to say I'm with 'em on that count. If I were to personify Lucifer it would by like this: Lucifer anchors the world of polarity and duality, basically the world of illusion or Maya as some cultures call it. And also Free Will, so we can have the experiences we chose to have here. He does what he does because we asked him to. An ungrateful job for sure since we don our veils, cross the river of forgetfulness and check in here with little to no memory of setting up this whole video game ourselves.

And in this personification, Lucifer, the Light Bearer, is there to catch us when we reach a low point. Even if we go so deep into darkness that we drop out the bottom, we still end up in a place of light, in the Light Bearer's arms. Hey, as long as we're dreaming things up and creating our own reality, how's about we make it a good one.

And associating Satan with Lucifer has never sat well with me either. The article *Some Light on Lucifer* by Ina Beldris had this to say:

> There is yet another reason why it makes no sense to read the Devil into Isaiah 14: the traditional role of Satan in the Old Testament. Satan comes from the Hebrew satan, which means "opponent" or "adversary." According to Strong's Concordance, this word appears in 1 Chronicles, Job, Psalms, and in Zechariah. In Psalms "satan" is used both in the plural (accusers) and in the indefinite sense (an accuser). In Chronicles and Zechariah its usage is ambiguous, while in Job "satan" as The Accuser appears only in the first two of its 42 chapters. It is important, however, to keep in mind that the texts of the Old Testament did not reach their "final" version until after the Babylonian exile. Before this exile there is no evidence in Hebrew scriptures of an Accuser as a force that opposes God, and even after the exile it is still doubtful. Though the story of Job is very old, its final version is dated after the exile, after the Hebrews came into contact with the dualist Zoroastrian religion with its god of good and its god of evil.

Yes, the dualist Zoroastrian religion. So we're talking from Persia (Iran), which is next to the area of Sumeria / Babylon (Iraq).

Now we're back to Enki and Enlil, who account for "God's" (more like gods') schizophrenia in the Old Testament, which may have been built, in part, from Sumerian texts if you trace it back far enough. Enlil was the one that wanted to use Enki's newly designed human beings as a slave race. He also very much wanted to keep humans in the dark about divinity, technology and pretty much anything beyond what the five senses can detect. So, ah yeah, I could see how the people living under that rule could view that as evil and also how Enlil could fit the role of "Satan" as "accuser" and "adversary."

Demonization of Feminine Energy and Mother Earth

Feminine energy has been demonized and that has resulted in a severe imbalance in the human race and our world. This is not something that just has a negative, harmful, disempowering affect on women, but on men also. Perhaps it has taken an even greater toll on men.

Leonard Schlain, in his book *The Alphabet Versus the Goddess,* discusses how cultures through the ages that took on an alphabetic language became more left-brained and henceforth, more patriarchal. Cultures that used symbology, pictures, icons and oral traditions maintained the right-brained feminine energy. The middle ages are an example of how losing literacy rejuvenated respect for women. The age of chivalry came about as alphabetic language faded and icons and imagery returned. Gives some reason as to why the "god(s)" of the Old Testament didn't want graven images around. That alone would stimulate right-brain activity and assist in restoring feminine energy and bring a more balanced state of being.

Credo Mutwa, in his interview with David Icke in the video *Reptilian Agenda,* gives another reason as to why "the gods" were not to be portrayed accurately in drawings or sculptures. If their physicality were portrayed accurately down through the ages, humans would know that "the gods" were neither human nor the one true God, but a different species / race.

Since the Garden of Eden, when the first Adamic race convinced the Eves of the second Adamic race to rebel against being the slaves they were genetically designed to be, the "rulers" of this world have demonized women and the feminine. With the feminine

27

energies being discouraged, out went balance. As we strive in this age to return the power of the feminine, I hope that we keep that word balance in mind. The answer to a patriarchy is not a matriarchy. Humans have already experienced a matriarchy and the patriarchy is, in part, a backlash to that. Let's stop swinging the pendulum and re-pair our human society, as in put the pairs together again - the masculine and feminine. It's not just about men and women working together. More profoundly, it's about re-pairing the masculine and feminine energy within each of us.

It's debatable whether Jesus or Mary Magdalen existed. What's important is the symbology in these character's stories. The symbology surrounding Jesus' life is most certainly not unique to him. Many researchers list out all the various characters who shared the same symbology. The Heyeokah Guru in the book *Adam and Evil* has some rather extensive lists. I love and respect David Icke's research and he feels Jesus did not exist and states that there is no documented evidence from the time that Jesus was supposed to have lived. Barbara Marciniak's Pleiadians claim that "Christ" was not one man, but was a consciousness embodied in many souls who came to Earth to assist in raising the frequency about the time when Jesus was supposed to have lived. (This is happening right now also.) There may be something to the stories of Jesus, but it may have been the stories of many souls compressed into the story of one man.

An astrologer friend of mine was reading a book making the case that Jesus did not exist. I had to chuckle. Astrologers talk about Roman deities all the time - Mercury, Venus, Mars, Jupiter, etc. In doing so, they are talking about the archetypal symbology to do with those characters and what it means on a personal level to their clients. I would highly doubt that many astrologers spend much time debating if these Roman deities actually existed or not. Why engage in a debate over whether Jesus and the myriad of other messiah characters, down through the ages, in numerous cultures worldwide, who shared his same life symbology, existed or not? That's a distraction from the real information contained in the symbology. The symbology is not merely about those characters it's about us. Look to such tales as a way of learning about yourself. What's in it for you? What is the original meaning behind this ancient symbology? What does it point to for the individual, earth-based human society, Earth, the solar system, and / or the Milky Way galaxy?

Even though the story of Jesus has been vastly corrupted from what it started as, even that corrupted version still has much to teach us. But I can see how the Roman Catholic Church has twisted the Jesus story to not only further the patriarchy, but to also promote the "down" side of the Age of Pisces, that being the whole victim / martyr / blame game. At this point in time, human society certainly has that down. And the up side of Piscean energy, such as intuition and connection to spirit, has been demonized and discouraged. I've known many men who were really very intuitive and if you told them that they'd go through the roof. Malcolm Gladwell, in his book *Blink,* often describes intuitive experiences, but, son of a gun if he'll call it that. To the contrary, he goes out of his way to say he is not describing such. These people know there's something to this, they witness and experience it themselves, but their conditioning is showing. They could stand to tuck that in.

Margaret Starbird is one who speaks of the Divine Feminine and the Sacred Union between masculine and feminine and how that is represented in the story of Mary Magdalen. Much of Dan Brown's novel The Da Vinci Code is based on Margaret's work. Margaret makes the case that Mary Magdalen was Jesus' bride. Now, especially if a bride of equal caliber to Jesus is involved, I can see the Catholic Church, that wanted to continue the imbalance of the patriarchy and the control that goes with that, destroying any evidence of a real Jesus' existence, which may be why David Icke and others can't find any if someone associated with that name did actually exist. I understand that the Vatican has 17 miles of underground library. Seems as though every time they had a book burning, they saved a few copies for themselves.

And if the Catholic Church and the Roman Empire wanted to continue the imbalance imposed by the patriarchy, they would take the story of Jesus' bride and greatest apostle, Mary Magdalen, and twist it and turn it and they did just that as they dared to label Mary Magdalen a prostitute. As Tom Kenyon and Judi Sion's book states, Mary Magdalen was not a prostitute, but was into sex magic, as was Mother Mary. Not only was Jesus teaching Mary, but she too was teaching him and she was sharing the power of her sex magic with him, helping to energize his Ka body (light body) for ascension after the crucifixion – if the crucifixion really happened. But ascension can happen, no literal, physical crucifixion necessary, although a crucifixion and resurrection or death and rebirth may take place on other levels, many times over, in the process of ascension. Here, again, I find it interesting, that even if Jesus and / or the crucifixion didn't actually take place, the symbology is still relevant.

Regardless of whether these characters were real people or not, it's obvious that the Jesus story had gained much momentum by the fourth century. It became a threat to the Romans and the Catholics. Constantine the Great and the Counsel of Nicea then went about the task of homogenizing all the information concerning such and also humankind's beginnings into one book called the Bible. This was done, as a bare minimum, to get everyone on the same sheet of music so that the masses were more easily controlled. The Romans and the Catholics both wanted to maintain control and couldn't stand heretics, which literally means, "one who thinks for themselves." Sounds criminal doesn't it? Eee gad. How dare anyone actually think for himself or herself?

Frankly, I so don't care if these characters existed or not. Either way is just not going to rock my world. There could be much debate over whether any of us actually exist or if we're just a figment of someone's imagination. I most certainly care about these characters' stories though. Like I said, this archetypal symbology is about US.

There is much self-knowledge to be gained there. Jesus said, "Have I not said ye are gods? You too shall do these and greater things." Perhaps if we look to this information with an eye to learning about ourselves we can finally return to being the Christs, gods, the soul resurrection machines we were designed to be.

Mother Earth herself has been demonized. The concept of humans being a steward of this world has seemingly been twisted and turned. Instead of meaning that we are responsible for her care, we instead seem to think we can literally have our way with her. Radio show host Art Bell once had said it'd be like placing a child in someone's care only to have them then molest that child. That's not what being a good steward is about.

On the topic of global warming, what we are doing to this planet on a physical level is horrific, but that doesn't hold a candle to the damage we've done on the energetic level. Like I keep saying, the energetic level is where it all starts, it's the most subtle and yet the most significant, the most powerful. The biggest issue here is our ignorance of what is currently going on in these significant times we find ourselves in. How Al Gore and his gang are addressing this whole global warming issue is yet another distraction to the truth. There's more than just the earth heating up. The sun and the whole solar system are heating up. Do you really think our car emissions are causing Jupiter to heat up? Richard Hoagland's (www.enterprisemission.com) hyperdimensional physics model tells of how we are witnessing the effects of a cause whose origin is in other dimensions that are currently beyond our senses to detect. All the solar system's celestial bodies are heating up, at a rate that is beyond what our intensifying sun is contributing. The planets are literally heating from the inside out.

Now, we get to the real reason why the Al Gores of the world want to provide us with a "if we only keep our noses to the grindstone, we can build a better car" distraction. The times we are in are not ordinary by any means. We are nearing the end of many cycles, including the Great Cycle, a 26,000-year precession of the equinoxes cycle. We are literally in a time of choosing between extinction and evolution. It's Arthur C. Clark and Stanley Kubrick's 2001: A Space Odyssey all over again. They, like so many others, are giving us the heads up. The Cosmos is sending us energy that, if tapped into, will mean a great evolutionary leap. If we don't do our inner work, these same cosmic rays and our own dysfunctional way of being can mean our destruction. Some outward evidence of the changes is increased solar activity and earth changes. Weather is extreme almost everywhere. Or had you noticed? Some folks still don't seem to know that this is going on. Perhaps denial is more than just a river in Egypt.

We've got to raise our frequency to ride this one out. We definitely have to tap into Love. Jesus (and how many others?) said to the establishment, "You have the information, you won't let anyone else have it and yet you don't know what to do with it yourself." The establishment is very fear motivated. They have done much to make the rest of us that way and have controlled us through our fears. And yet Love is the answer. Literally. And "they" just don't get that. Yep, they may have all the tools and information and technology, but they don't know how to use Love with all that. They have spent too much time living in the vibration of Fear. They could read this, chuckle, then get right back to looking for their next adrenaline rush.

Demonization of Psychedelic Drugs

First of all, we gotta look at the meaning of the word psychedelic. The word psychedelic is an English term coined from the Greek words for "soul" (psyche), and "manifest" (delos). Keep this word origin / original vibration of this word in mind as you read on.

Natural, psychedelic drugs have been utilized for millennia by many cultures as a way to extract a whole lot of useful information from our home realm of spirit. Hemp, magic mushrooms, ayawaska, etc., have been and still are used by tribal peoples. Here, again, if you understand that the "rulers" of this world want us to be mind-controlled slaves, then you can easily see why these natural drugs are so demonized. Anything linking us to spirit, to our true selves, to Christ Consciousness, is not something they want us to delve into.

Our seven main chakras each have a gland associated with them. Our pituitary gland is associated with the crown chakra. Our pineal gland is associated with the third eye chakra. These glands are where "altered states" happen, whether those altered states come through spiritual meditation / visualization, energy work, sex or the use of psychedelic drugs. All of these break down the "barrier" around the pituitary and allow for connection to spirit.

Check into Terrance McKenna's work (and so many others) for the revelations about our human existence that have been achieved through psychedelic drugs.

Don't confuse these natural adventures into spirit with the psychotropic drugs promoted by psychiatry, the pharmaceutical industry and the FDA. Ancient and tribal people and folks like Terrance have pursued such with the intention of enlightenment. And when I say "natural" I do mean natural. There are many plants and even animals that provide the chemicals necessary to switch our pituitary and pineal glands on to connecting to spirit. These same chemicals are produced in our own bodies and spiritual enlightenment processes can and will produce the same effects. These psychodelics can give us a heads up, if you will, to that experience.

At the other extreme, Big Pharma and their cohorts are literally abusing their power and influence to strike it rich and to control and kill people through the use of psychotropic drugs. Unfortunately, they are doing a pretty good job on all those counts. We're not talking about a one-time or occasional intentional, spiritual journey, but a lifelong dangerous, controlling prescription to dysfunction, ill health and literally death. The same kind of drug testing that occurred in the Nazi concentration camps has been taken to the unwitting general public in a grand crime against humanity. See the movie *Making a Killing – The Untold Story of Psychotropic Drugging.* Also check into the history of I.G. Farben (that morphed into Bayer) and their activities at Auschwitz for more information about the intent behind such testing then and now.

Demonization of Expression of Emotion

I'm a very passionate person about finding the truth of things. I've called myself a truth seeker for years. A couple years ago, I learned that, astrologically speaking, the decan (10 day period of the 30 days of a sun sign) I was born in says just that - I'm a truth seeker. In talking with folks, sharing different perspectives that are so far from mainstream that it usually knocks someone's socks off, my passion will kick in and I get all fired up. I've had folks ask me why I'm so angry. First of all, they say "angry," as if it's a bad thing. If I actually were angry, I'd probably have to say, "Thanks for noticing." There is much to be angry about in this world. A friend of mine says the quote about "If you're not outraged, you're not paying attention." The only bad emotions are those that are not expressed. ALL of our emotions have a message for us. It would serve us not to ignore or stuff ANY of our emotions.

The vast majority of the time though, this comment comes when I'm not angry. I most certainly have experienced and definitely know what anger feels like. It is most certainly different than passion. Why do people perceive passion as anger? Do they see all intense emotion as anger? What's their trigger that makes them mistake one for the other? This reminds me of one of the Four Agreements (www.miguelruiz.com) - don't take things personally, as what others say and do is a projection of their own reality. This type of projection, seeing passion as anger, often comes from folks who are so very expressionless you feel like checking their vital signs, "Anybody in there?" Makes me wonder what emotions of all sorts are they stuffing, suppressing. Sounds like those Pink Floyd lyrics, "I have become comfortably numb."

> *We're too busy keeping our emotions in check to ever dream of infinite possibilities. And maybe that is the ultimate conspiracy.*

> *Ramtha from the movie What the Bleep!? Down the Rabbit Hole*

The Pleiadians tell us in Barbara Marciniak's book *Bringers of the Dawn*, our emotions are our road, bridge or ticket to our spiritual selves.

People will assign "good" and "bad" judgment to emotions. We can even get to the point of squelching those so-called "good" emotions like Love. Love is a very powerful force and if suppressed, kept inside, it can burn us up from the inside out. Bottling up our love can result in chronic illness just as easily as bottling up rage and anger. Again, the only bad emotions are the ones that are not expressed.

Demonization of Money

This one ought to be a little obvious, but, just like with any other brainwashing, the brainwashed don't know they are. At a conscious level, we may think we don't have an attitude towards money, and yet many do due to childhood programming and lifelong conditioning. Most people can't deny the power money holds in this world on the mundane level. And yet in a conditioned, disempowered state, one's feelings of unworthiness can make them repel money instead of attract it. Having wealth is often felt to be for someone else or a far off, perhaps unachievable dream. And even those who actually attract money can often find all sorts of ways to quickly get rid of it, often on things that are of no importance or, worse yet, that are not healthy at some level.

A while back, I met someone online. We didn't talk much online and arranged to meet in person. The first part of the conversation started with what we do for a living. This person had been an accountant and now was working with homeless people. I said I had just started a life-coaching business. This person immediately asked me how could I justify asking that much money for such services. There had been no mention of what I was asking for payment. They lashed out at me over their personal issues with money, which in no way could have anything to do with me, as they had known me all of five minutes. Later, I told them that I didn't care to have them in my life, as they obviously had personal issues with money. What I could not afford was to be around someone who had a "money is evil" attitude, as I was just starting a new business and my lifelong career had seemingly abandoned me years ago and I was feeling fairly sure at the time that it was never to return.

I also found it interesting that this person went from being an accountant to helping homeless folks. This money thing was part of the life lesson they had chose to experience this go 'round. I told them I would rather help people heal and grow than to become another one of this person's "clients," meaning I didn't care to become homeless myself by not supporting myself. I also told them that the last thing homeless people need is "money is evil" energy.

There's the saying, "money is the root of all evil." Here, again, comes the brainwashing that something powerful is evil. This is one reason why the Global Elite have peddled Jesus as being a poor carpenter. In order to be good, you must be penniless. And if being almost penniless is good enough for Jesus Christ, by God, it's good enough for you. Here, again, if something has power, it's demonized in hopes that those who don't want to be "evil" won't use it. Many Joe Averages do manage to tap into money, but there's a whole lot who are totally removed from the game, totally gutted as far as using the power of money for good just because they've been brainwashed to think it's evil.

Again, there is nothing inherently good or evil in this world. It depends upon the intent behind it. Kevin Trudeau, in his book *Natural Cures "They" Don't Want You to Know About*, talks about the corruption and agenda of the FDA, the FTC, pharmaceutical companies, the health care system, etc. Not much of what he said is news to me, nor can I argue with much of it. I'm glad that someone who has as much exposure as himself is getting this word out... finally. But he says this agenda is all about the money. I disagree. Money is a means to an end. The global elite certainly use money as a means to their end. The intent behind their agenda is control. It's about control!

Trudeau says it's the "love" of money that is the issue, the evil. He said that, in this world, money is loved and people are used, when it should be the other way around. Well, yes, people could use some love most definitely and yet it's ok to use people, just don't ab-use them. And money could stand to be used for something beneficial to us all, but I just don't like that message of saying that loving money is wrong. Here's the "either / or" choice that need not be. Why can't you love people without ab-using them and still love money? If you hate, or shun or treat money (or anything) as evil, why would you expect this power tool to come to you? If it did come to you in that state of mind, why would you use it for good, when you've been brainwashed to think it's evil? And if you'd like to use this power tool for good, how CAN you use it if you don't have it?

If Trudeau truly thinks this is all about money, he is missing the true agenda behind all of this. He certainly is seeing the effects from all this and how our health is paying for it. And THAT is the whole idea. It's not that "they" don't care about our health. They very much do. They WANT us to have poor health. It's not a side effect from their desires for profit that we just HAPPEN to lose our health. It is in their control agenda to MAKE EVERY EFFORT to get us to lose our health. As a simple example, why does refined sugar, which is just empty carbs without the nutrients to utilize those carbs, cost less than raw sugar, which is whole and healthy and has had very little processing done to it?! Why does a processed product, something that has had time and labor put into it, cost less than something that's not had that additional time and labor put into it?! Does the thing that is not healthy for us cost less because we're being lead through our money (or seeming lack thereof) to buy and consume it instead of the healthy thing that costs more? Are they taking a loss on such "food" products in order to influence our choices? It's rather tough to be gods or Christs when we aren't even fueling our bodies properly. It's far easier to keep people down who are unhealthy.

Just like in George Orwell's *1984*, the label on institutions can often be just the opposite of what it's truly about. In *1984*, the Ministry of Peace dealt with war. The Ministry of Plenty dealt with rationing. The Ministry of Truth dealt with re-writing history to make it match current conditions. In the "real" world, the FDA approves the products of institutions that often do more harm than good to our health. Religions have in some cases done more for keeping us from spirit than helping us connect to it. The World Wildlife Federation, who is supposed to be in charge of helping save endangered species, sets up restricted areas where Joe Average would literally be shot if found there and yet the global elite will go into these areas... and do what? Hunt endangered species.

The global elite have all the money they could possibly wish for. Oftentimes, that's "old money" that's passed through many generations of "bloodline" families by this time. They're swimming in it. It's not as if they need more. Kevin Trudeau mentions a lot of the same things I do - a messed up food industry, a messed up health care system, legal drug pushers, the automobile industry buying out other options to keep their monopoly, etc. All of these things are harmful to us and to our planet. If it were purely about profit, well, there's plenty enough money could be made off of beneficial industries. Why don't the global elite tap into legalizing hemp and replacing all the toxic industries with it and do it all safer and more efficiently and effectively? Why don't the global elite tap into alternative medicine? Why don't they start an alternative mode of transportation? They have all the resources to jump out into the lead with all these things. They could advertise, market, set up stores far easier than the next person but, hey, that stuff is actually beneficial to us and the planet. Can't have that. It would serve us to get to the nitty gritty of why these things go on in this world and it's not out of sheer greed. All that money might be a nice side effect for them and a powerful tool for them to use, but it's not the main motivation.

Now as you go down the hierarchy, you may very well run into people who do things just for the money. Their brainwashing is showing. This is the world they were born into. This is how they've been raised. This is how they've been conditioned. They don't know the agenda at the top. They're too caught up in the system, too caught up in the brainwashing, too caught up in busy-busy.

They've bought into the addiction, the obsession. It's all they know. They are unwitting pawns being used. If they actually would pull their heads up long enough to take a look around and research what really goes on in this world, they'd quit participating in their own enslavement. And that's exactly why so many are running at such a frantic, hectic pace. It's part of the global control agenda to keep people too busy to take any time to see what's really going on in this world. And so the cycle continues, the dog chases its tail.

The people at the very top of world control absolutely know what their agenda is about - keep down the human race, who, if left to their natural way of being, would be gods and Christs. Again, like William Henry said, Christs don't pay their taxes. Christs are not very controllable. And "they" have made it a full time job to keep us down. They have to. Without the constant barrage of psychic abuse, brainwashing and propaganda, we'd be just that - left to our natural way of being. Our inner voice and knowingness would, in fairly short order, prompt us to be a truer version of ourselves. We wouldn't end up in a disempowered state... without "their" constant psychic tamperings.

There's an awful lot of good we can do in this world that doesn't involve money, but, as things are presently, money does have great power in this world. How's about those of us who care about this world and its inhabitants start shifting our energy to draw money to us rather than repel it. Louise Hay's *Receiving Prosperity* can be of help in this area. Louise discusses how we create our own reality when it comes to money. Our feelings about money affect how we receive it. Just like with other areas of our lives, the "programming" of our feelings about money happens at a young age. If you think you have to work hard to have your needs met, then you do. If you feel making money is a breeze, it will flow to you and it will feel effortless... and that's ok. Score. How we feel about money in general will determine if it stays in our lives. Some people can get a bonus or an inheritance or win the lottery and still not have much of anything because they have the energy that they are not worthy of having that money. They will literally dream up ways to give it away, or spend it on useless things, just some way to get rid of it.

Let's put that power tool called money to use to turn this world around. The "other side" is using it, why don't we?

Demonization of All Things Healthy

People have gotten conditioned to think, like this person I use as an example in the beginning of the last section, that spending any amount of time, money or effort on anything good for you is too much spent. I've been eating organic food for many years now. I'll have people comment on how healthy I look. People around my own age can't believe I'm as old as I am. I'll tell them I eat whole, organic food and they immediately say, "that's too expensive." I'll tell them that, for starters, not all organic food is more expensive than its conventional counterpart. And even if it is more expensive, it's not that much more... so, pay now or pay later. You can pay your grocer for healthy food that isn't laden with manmade chemical toxins, that actually has nutrients in it – ya know, the whole reason for eating in the first place, or you can pay your western medicine doctor far more and they may never help you. And, if they don't get you back into the fundamentals of whole, organic food, you've not addressed the fundamental physical level cause of your health problems.

But, like I've said throughout, it all starts at the energy level. The mental, emotional state of "that's too much to spend on food", ya know, for me, 'cause I'm not worthy' is the real beginning of the problem. The diet and lifestyle choices that follow are just in keeping with that energy. So, yes, like the person in the last section, many folks think anything healthy at any level is not worth the time, money or effort. Any counselors, therapists, coaches, healers, dieticians, massage practitioners, etc., just want too much money for the healing and growth help they offer. But those same folks who think this way think nothing of spending any amount of money on doctors or insurance or for a latte or an alcoholic drink, or endless money on cigarettes, gambling, drugs, and material things they rarely have time to use since they are slaving so hard to pay for it all. But, for goodness sakes, don't spend one thin dime on something that could actually be of some healing and growth benefit. As Neale Donald Walsch wrote about in his *Conversations With God* series of books, our thoughts, words and deeds are not always in line with our goals. Ain't Free Will fun? Most folks say they want to be happy and healthy and yet their choices lead them in a different direction. If one continues down the path they're on, they'll get to where they're going.

The interesting thing is, if we do what is fundamentally healthy, we won't pay as much in time, money or effort in the long run. The real answers are just based on re-learning what we've forgotten about fundamental health and living. It's about getting the right information and then applying that to your life.

Dr. Lorraine Day learned the hard way about health and lack thereof. She developed breast cancer and almost died. What her experiences as a doctor did teach her is that conventional medicine does not cure cancer. So when she got cancer herself, she knew she had to do something different. Since she was literally starting from her almost death bed, it was a long haul, but she climbed out of that pit to regain her health. That was over a decade ago.

I tell people that proper diet and lifestyle is no harder to maintain than an improper way of being, but, after a lifetime of getting it wrong, the change itself may be challenging. It doesn't help much that society in its highly conditioned state has not been so supportive of a healthy diet and lifestyle. But the more of us that change, put our money and energies towards the fundamentals that work, that make demands on society to change (such as grocery stores and restaurants) and literally learning more ourselves, the faster things will turn around. Just learning things ourselves puts that information out into the collective conscious. It's the 100th monkey effect. Enough of us change and the tide will turn.

For two very good free video interviews with Dr. Lorraine Day, go to CMN, Conscious Media Network. Lorraine was 69 the day of those interviews and she looks great and said she has the energy of a 25-year-old.

Suzanne Somers was promoting a natural menopause medication. The gal she gets it from is an anthropologist by trade who had a TV interview and the interviewer asked her what qualified her to make this medication since she was not a "medical" practitioner of some sort. She said, "I don't need a license to think." Ha! Indeed. We've gotten to the point where we think we have to be licensed or degreed or certified by someone else. It's like being knighted. Someone doth dub thee... whatever. Why does someone else's opinion of our "knowledge" make or break how credible it is? As I see it, many folks who do have umpteen degrees and certifications and licenses have been indoctrinated into a way of being that excludes thinking. Most regurgitate what they were taught in many years of school or perhaps many years of church going and they never question whether the information they've been slathered in is valid or worthwhile. "Hey, it's what I learned in school. It's what the preacherman said. It's all I've ever known. That makes it a fact... right?" So-called experts often tout their information as facts, even though those so-called facts are constantly proven to be untrue.

What all of us have to offer each other is an opinion, a perspective. But the "experts" with various letters after their names and degrees upon their walls are often purporting their information as fact. It would serve each and every one of us to maintain responsibility of our own lives, to be our own authority, our own "expert." Taking in other perspectives is VERY valuable, but we are all the final and ultimate test of the truth for ourselves. Don't let some highly brainwashed, indoctrinated soul be your authority, calling the shots for your life. First, pay attention to your own inner voice - does the information presented resonate with you? Then the ultimate test is to put things to the test. Apply their wisdom to your life and see what it does for you. And like Einstein said, the definition of insanity is doing the same thing over and over and expecting different results. If your present life choices are not getting you to your goals, then have you considered that what you are doing, thinking, emoting, believing doesn't work and perhaps it's the wrong direction? Attempt something different if you already know your present way of being isn't working.

It would serve us to acknowledge that we don't need liaisons to wisdom or to spirit. The priestly caste used to serve and still serve as liaisons, go-betweens between God and us. Now doctors serve as our priests in health and act as the liaison between our health and us. Who the hell are they? No really. Why are we giving authority of our lives over to someone we interact with for a few minutes of our lives? Doctors and dentists are a great example on this one since they are lucky to live past their 50s since they are practicing what they preach. How much of a health expert are they when they can't even live long to tell about it?

Our direct connection to spirit and to the "All Knowing" is inward. Yes, indeed, other perspectives can be most useful, to expose us to new ways of looking at things, especially when we've been in a world that has conditioned us to doubt our own inner voice. I'd be in a world of hurt if I didn't draw on my fellow human's perspective, knowledge and experiences. So, yes, draw on other information from your fellow human, then be your own ultimate test, run it past your intuition and feel for resonance. And then speak your own truth. What the next person does with it is up to them.

Demonization of God

Yep. You heard that right. That's the next thing to demonize. The extreme right presents such a horrid version of God that they are essentially driving people from God. The extreme left seems to want to just flat erase God.

On the Comedy Channel, standup comedians cannot say "Jesus Christ" without it being censored. They may be using it as an exclamation, but, nevertheless if said on the Comedy Channel, it gets censored.

A few years back, John Travolta was on Ellen. I'd inadvertently (synchronistically perhaps?) taped this show. They showed a clip of John's latest film. At one point, a character said, "God damned." Well, it got censored out. If I couldn't rewind and re-listen, I'd have wondered if I'd heard what I had really heard. Sure enough. What was censored was "God" not "damned." And I know that "damn" is not a word that is censored on TV. South Park plays on this all the time. They say cuss words, which get censored, but they say damn often and it never gets censored. I can't help but think they do this, in part, to point out the fact that "damn" is not censored on TV.

We are all gods. We have the power to bless or to damn. I'll use the 'f' word long before I go around willy-nilly damning things. Where most people would say, "God damn it", I say, "God bless it." And I am well aware of my intention when I do. Every situation is here for our experience and our spiritual growth... God bless it anyway!

ACCEPT AND ALLOW - LETTING GO OF CONTROL

I was watching the TV Series "Bones." A Catholic cemetery was blown out of the ground by a bursting water main. In the process of identifying bodies, they found a murder victim. The character of

Bones speaks very straight across to people. In the process of the investigation, Bones, being rather science minded (she has her own dogma), expressed some opinions that were not in line with Catholic doctrine and, henceforth, not politically correct considering who was in earshot. The elderly priest thought that Bones was making fun of consecrated ground. FBI agent Booth, who works with Bones, is chewing her a new one (Booth is obviously Catholic). She goes 'round with him and finally tells him, "Can't you just be satisfied that if I'm wrong about God I'll burn in Hell?"

We often get so caught up in trying to control everything in our lives. We try to control other people and shape and mold them into something they aren't in an attempt to make them into something we want. I heard it said once, "A marriage license is not a sculptor's license." The same would apply to any form of relationship. I've flat told people that I'd appreciate it if they didn't put my face on their fantasy.

And we attempt to control situations just as much. How many times have you been through what you relatively / judgmentally call a tough experience only to realize the very profound lessons involved with that. Here we are handed gifts, opportunities for growth and we want to control it, fight it, resist it. And it is the resistance to that experience that is causing our pain, not the experience itself. If we did our best to flow with the experiences Life presents to us, even if the ride gets a bit bumpy, it still doesn't hurt like it does when we resist. There are two ways to get somewhere, either voluntarily or kicking and screaming. You can bet that if Life and your Higher Self want you to have a certain experience, you will have it. If you go voluntarily, you'll not only get through it quicker, you'll also not rip yourself up as much as when you dig your heels in the whole way.

A friend saw a young, very enlightened Buddhist give a talk. One of the topics was this desire to control everything. He joked that perhaps we could start small and just give the Universe 60 / 40.

We all come here to have experiences. Who are we to tell others they cannot have the experiences they came to have? Who are we to judge what is right or wrong for someone else? Compassion is not the same as pity or sorrow. We can show love and compassion for someone without denying them the very

43

experiences they came to have, even if somewhere along the way we relatively / judgmentally deem their experiences as negative or painful. We can offer them another way to look at things, ask them to consider another way of being, but, if they are bound and determined to have their experience, then let them. It's back to the demonization of mistakes. Out of fear of making mistakes, we stop living. We didn't come here to not live or to not experience. Live spelled backwards is evil. Live already. But if your way of life makes you miserable, you might consider changing.

Some of the toughest situations in which we humans have difficulty letting go of the desire to control are ones where we don't even have anything at personal stake ourselves, the situations where someone else is choosing to experience something that comes with a lot of pain and suffering. Perhaps they are allowing themselves to stay in an abusive situation or one where someone is controlling them or they make choices in self-abuse such as all manner of addictions, etc., the list goes on. As much as we may feel for them, we cannot make their choices for them. Not only is it not our place to do so, it's just flat impossible to do so, without perhaps hog-tying them. Who the hell are we to tell someone they can't have the experiences they are choosing to have? We all have enough to do without taking on the burden of someone else's drama.

Emotional Freedom Technique (EFT) that I talk about under Our Beliefs as Our Environment offers an example of how acknowledging and accepting what is can actually change those things. An affirmation of an issue which then ends with "... but I still love and accept myself" is used to make the previously stated issue go away. Simply amazing. There's much to be gained from acceptance.

As the Buddhists say, "Everything is as it should be." Let go, let God. Trust the process. For everything there is a season, and a time for every purpose under Heaven. Our mistakes are teaching us.

Having said all this, allowing others to have the experiences they are choosing to have does not mean you have to participate in those experiences with them. It doesn't mean you even have to be around them. Maybe shooting heroine just isn't your thing. Well, extreme example, but you get the idea.

And sometimes even those folks that we once shared experiences with, we sometimes part ways with. Perhaps we've had enough of that before they have had their fill. It's time for us to move on. Not that we love them any less, we just don't care to have those experiences any longer. We cannot hold ourselves back just because they aren't ready yet. The senior class has to graduate and move on. They still love the juniors, but it serves no one for them to stay back when it's time they take on new adventures.

On the flip side of things, I've known plenty of so-called enlightened folks who think they can judge when someone else is ready to hear something or experience something. They judge that the next person is not ready, so will not share a tidbit of wisdom with them. I've told people I will send Reiki, healing lifeforce energy, to people without asking them on the conscious level. Oh, my God, they act like I just murdered someone. "You shouldn't violate their free will like that." As if I could. We can't violate each other's Free Will. I'm not saying can't as in *shouldn't,* but that we are not *able* to. It's not possible to do so. We can share information and healing energy with anyone at any time and they can either do something with it or not. Again, who the hell are we to judge whether they are ready for it or not. They and their higher selves will take it to mind and heart... or not.

ALTRUISM

Let's start this topic out with some dictionary definitions. I find it interesting that many dictionaries seem to have a definition of altruism for animals being different than for humans. Here's one example:

> *1 : unselfish regard for or devotion to the welfare of others*
>
> *2 : behavior by an animal (why an animal? my question) that is not beneficial to or may be harmful to itself but that benefits others of its species*

Another put the second definition this way:

2. Zoology - Instinctive cooperative behavior that is detrimental to the individual but contributes to the survival of the species.

Here's another definition:

willingness to do things that benefit other people, even if it results in disadvantage for yourself.

I think that at this stage of the game of life, we have created even another definition: willingness to do things that we THINK benefits others, when it really doesn't, but boy does it sure mess us up in the process.

Heart sang a song called Black on Black, in which were these lyrics, "The oldest story known to man, the willing sacrificial lamb." We've been conditioned to "sacrifice" ourselves even when it's NOT benefitting others or society at large. Making a sacrifice for something? Well, ok. But for nothing?

I've heard people say, "I'm giving So & So everything I can." Perhaps that's just it - that's not the answer. Perhaps we could stand to self-nurture, to tend to our own needs first. We'd be not only making sure that at least one person in this world is taken care of, but we would also be setting a good example. Here's someone who understood the conditioning we've all been subjected to:

Few things are harder to put up with than the annoyance of a good example. - Mark Twain

Sad state that is – that a good example would cause annoyance but I most certainly have witnessed that.

Motion is not always indicative of progress. A dog chasing its tail isn't getting anywhere. These days, people are often running themselves into the ground being so concerned about others. If we sacrifice enough of ourselves, we are not only of no use to this world we are harming it more. A good example is chronic illness. If we wear ourselves down to the point of having no energy for even ourselves, we surely have nothing for anyone else and we instead become a burden upon others. Someone then has to become our caretaker. And if we take it to the point of passing from this life, well, we won't be here any longer to be serving this realm.

Take care of yourself, maintain yourself. We have to LIVE here to help here. It's a matter of priorities. Take care of you FIRST. It's just like the flight attendant telling you to put on your oxygen mask first before helping someone with his or hers. You won't be much help to others if you can't breathe.

I saw an article online once about stopping the aid to Africa. The gist of this article was that this aid often arrives in the form of giving a fish rather than teaching to fish. People are discouraged from finding their own way, making their own livelihood, tapping into their own creativity, etc., and are conditioned to take the handout or the global corporate job rather than have their own small businesses or farms, etc. (Gee, Africa sounds a lot like America.) In effect. they are disempowered and dependent. They are "kept", nothing better than slaves to the system. (Wait, are we taking about America again?!)

Along with this is delivered the attitude of "they're lucky to have these things", as if any problems they may have had magically left their lives upon colonization. Not. It's like the ego of a parent who thinks that they know what's best for their children for their entire lives, not just during childhood when the child could use their help, support and guidance. Sometimes our idea of "help" really isn't helping, it's harming.

If you truly want to help others, help them to be more self-reliant, self-sufficient and less dependent on you or anyone else. Empower others. The best way to teach this is by example. Be more self-reliant, self-sufficient and less dependent yourself. Tap into your own personal power and shine that light to the world in your everyday goings on. And none of this excludes helping one another when someone could use a hand. These ways of being that start with "self" are the very things that enable us to be of the MOST help to this world and its inhabitants.

The cinch part of this is that if we get our priorities straight, start with self in every way, address the "in here" part, then we'll be doing the "out there" part with no effort. With every breath we take and every move we make, we'll exude all that love, respect, nurturing, compassion, peace, and calm we conjured up for ourselves to a world that could use it as much as we each do ourselves. And no matter where you go, there you are. You don't have to go looking for someone to practice on, you're right here, always. Practice on yourself. Take care of yourself.

EITHER / OR VS. AND / BOTH

It may also serve us to get out of the concept of "either / or." The TV show South Park related this idea in their typically comical way. There is an occasional character on South Park named Towelie. Towelie is a genetically enhanced towel that the military originally developed as a weapon, "Can you imagine being drier than dry?" Well, Towelie was one of the earlier attempts at this genetic enhancement and he has a few "defects". One of these is that he's a pot head. Yep, a weed-smoking towel. Kinda sounds like a fire hazard, eh? Well, in one episode, Towelie and the kids of South Park are back at his birthplace of Tynecorp. The kids are in trouble and literally hanging by a thread. Towelie has the opportunity to save them, but another "evil" enhanced towel is tempting him with a joint, "Which do you choose?" Towelie looks back and forth between the kids and the joint and says, "I choose, I choose... both!" and stretches out one arm to grab the kids and the other to grab the joint.

Life oftentimes isn't really about "either / or" but instead it is "and / both." We can help ourselves OR we can help others? Why only have one of those when we can have both?

Also people have gotten into the mode of thinking that we often only have choices between having a "bad" thing (or a "bad" version of it) or not having anything at all. The internal combustion engine is a good example of this. Here we are in a self-proclaimed "advanced, progressive" society and yet we're still motoring around with a century old technology. 100 years old! It's amazing to think that anyone would believe there are no other viable options. This demonstrates how controlled such areas of our lives are. There have been and still are many alternate and viable ways of transportation and those environmentally safer ways can still allow for the independence we desire from personal vehicles.

Another example of "bad" or nothing is cell phones. Cell phone technology has gotten MORE dangerous to our health through the new generations of technology, not less so. The older analog cell phones were higher power, but used a constant carrier wave. This means that in the analog phones what our bodies "feel" is that continuous constant carrier wave. It has the voice signal mixed in with it, but there is not much change in what our bodies perceive when there is voice signal there or when there isn't. Newer digital phones have lower overall power output but are pulsed - there is only transmission signal when there is voice signal, so it's either flat line or BANG, there's signal, then BANG again down to flat line. It is that abrupt change in output that is harmful to us. Even though more high power, the analog phones were less harmful. And the 1996 Telecommunications Act set up the "push" to riddle the landscapes and cityscapes with cell phone antennas. This act proclaims that any argument against the installation of these towers cannot include health as a reason. And yet health is the VERY reason why most folks would not want an antenna near their home slowly cooking them with microwave energy.

Like I've said throughout this book, the energetic level is the most subtle and yet the most significant, the most powerful. Oftentimes, the more subtle, the more significant. The same is true for harmful energy also. When it was first discovered that microwaves could be used to cook was when technicians used to work on big microwave dish antennas while the dish was still powered on. Some technicians realized that they felt warm or the chocolate bar in their shirt pocket melted suddenly. If we were all bombarded with that level of microwave energy, we would be more likely to notice it and demand a stop to it. But cell antennas, both on the towers and in your phone, put out enough to go fairly unnoticed, and yet it works on you slowly but surely over time to cause damage to your body.

And yet the PR on the newer technology states they're better because they are lower power. Talk about deception. When explaining this to folks I'll get, "Well, it's so good to have the communication capability." Why, yes, it is. But this technology doesn't have to be harmful. Here again, folks have been bamboozled into thinking that we either have the harmful technology or nothing at all. It doesn't have to be this way. I really had to chuckle at the end of the movie *Thanks for Smoking* when the public relations man for the tobacco industry lost his job due to the truth coming out about how unhealthy tobacco is. His next job? PR for the cell phone industry. Ha!

In the food industry, they want to put what Dogtor J, John B. Symes, D.V.M. calls the Four Horsemen of the Apocalypse into everything. These four things are soy, dairy, gluten and corn. These are the top four "food" (use that term loosely) allergens and yet you're hard pressed to avoid them. So then they've got folks thinking it's either this or starve to death. Nope. Doesn't need to be that way. We've got no business eating these things, most especially in the quantities people are consuming them. If you don't label read, you probably aren't aware of how much of this stuff gets put into prepackaged food.

All four of these things have what is called casein in them, which is what industrial strength glues are made from. That's why there's a cow on the Elmer's Glue label – it's made from milk. Casein coats the duodenum (the first part of the small intestine) and, henceforth, blocks the absorption of nutrients from our foods. Normally, the duodenum is where we absorb the bulk of the nutrients from our food. These "foods" also pose other dangers, including containing hormones. Those who know they can't tolerate these so-called foods are really the lucky ones, as they know to avoid them. Others are getting poisoned slowly over time. See Dogtor J's article *Food Intolerance in Animals and Man*. (www.dogtorj.net/id1.html) Might I suggest that if you feel an urge to eat one or more of the Four Horsemen, that you do it in small amounts and hours away from eating other food, so as not to waste the nutrient content of the other food you eat.

Another issue that falls under this topic is how we have handled, or mishandled, monogamy. Monogamy is something that could stand to be done by choice. It should not be forced, not by societal rules, not by other, not by self. Perfectly good relationships are destroyed because people allow themselves to be forced into monogamy. The conditioning of "either / or" dictates that you cannot have more than one lover. If you have a lover and someone else comes along that you have a romantic energetic connection with, then the "either / or" mentality forces a choice that shouldn't have to be made. That mentality makes you think that to indulge in the second relationship means a definite end to the first. Many a good relationship has ended needlessly due to this strict adhesion to forced monogamy.

It's conditional

Not for free
There are strings attached
Tied to me
I'll want something back
If you agree
To be in love with me

Lyrics from "Conditional" by Tracy Chapman

It doesn't have to be this way. Don't get me wrong, if monogamy is for YOU, then fine. If it's not, then why are you forcing it on yourself? And you certainly have no business forcing it onto anyone else or to even think that you can, that you're able. Why have "either / or" when you can have "and / both."

Again, don't get me wrong. Like I said before, there is a great energy exchange during sex. Whether you're single or in partnership, it may not serve you to do just anything because it moved. Don't confuse drama with excitement and don't mistake stupidity for freedom. If you willy-nilly have sex with just anyone that's willing, you may be taking on energy that is anything but freeing. If we all had it together, had taken care of our issues, addressed our healing, then the free love movement of the 60s could be one fantastic reality, but do I really need to tell you that, for the most part, we're not quite there yet? A little sense and balance might be nice.

I had a friend who was seeing someone, but was also rather hung up on an ex. Their current lover told them they had no problem with them having sex with their ex, but that current lover wouldn't be having sex with them for three days afterward. Good for them. There's that "on the third day you'll rise again" thing. They were insisting that their sex partner clear some energy rather than pass it on to them.

I've heard it said that at this point in our evolution (or perhaps lack thereof) monogamy works for humans because we lack honesty and integrity in other forms of relationships. Excuse me, but I'm seeing a definite lack of honesty and integrity in so-called monogamous relationships. So-called. Many couples consist of one person saying they are and having a monogamous relationship, and another person saying that also, but not really having one.

51

Sometimes neither is monogamous and neither is honest about it. Seems to me we've rather screwed that one up also if it's lacking honesty and integrity. Sorry, but lip service is just not the real deal. Perhaps we could stand to realign our priorities. Instead of forcing monogamy, perhaps we could first work on being honest and insisting on honesty. Start by being honest with yourself. And honesty doesn't come by punishing someone when they are honest. And it doesn't come from telling our loved ones what we think they want to hear. It doesn't come from not giving the other the chance to absorb our honesty, to assume we know how they will respond to our honesty before we've been honest. My question is why does anyone want their lover to lie to them? Why does anyone want to lie to their lover? We've demonized another aspect of sexual love by living a lie, kidding ourselves about our sexuality, and by tolerating dishonesty from our lovers and ourselves.

And while we're on the topic of sex, just a re-minder, as in put your mind back into it... there are physical, nutritional reasons behind this also, but, gentlemen, if you need Viagra and ladies, if you need lube, on an energetic level do you think that maybe, just maybe, you really aren't supposed to be having sex with this person? And that may not have to do with them, maybe it's about you, maybe it's about timing or situation, etc., but listen to your body already.

The two party political system is another "either / or" that need not be. In this case, it's not that I care to see both in office, but both the hell out of there already. Goodness sakes, but that's just an illusion of choice, a choice between a rock and a hard place. They are so in cahoots it's not even funny.

Dr. Heather Anne Harder ran for U.S. President in 1996 and 2000. I heard about her during the 2000 campaign. Due to the obvious dysfunction in the political system, I've been mostly apolitical. Well, Heather's message was so awesome I couldn't help but get involved in her grass roots campaign. She's a very independent thinker and many independent and third-parties asked her to be their candidate. She ran on the Democratic ticket claiming to be a Jeffersonian Democrat. I can't help but think that a bigger, perhaps more accurate reason she did so was because she knew that she'd have to jump through more hoops if she didn't claim to be Democrat or Republican. Of course, the Democratic party did not endorse her. She was far too progressive a thinker for that and she wasn't playing by the rules. One is supposed to come up through local and state political offices before even dreaming about a federal position, let alone the presidency. That's how they indoctrinate people who perhaps had very noble political beginnings.

Heather and her supporters learned about how the playing field is anything but level. The two parties have the advantage over independent and third parties. One example of this is, in some states, a candidate that is not endorsed by the Republicans or Democrats (Republicrats or Democans) have to have petitions signed to have their name put on the ballot. If claiming to be a Republican or Democrat, they may need 1000 petition signatures. If of another party they may need 10,000 petition signatures. And that's just one example.

Under the Republicans, man oppresses man. Under the Democrats it's just the opposite. - Bumper sticker.

There are many other areas where we have drawn an "either / or" line that need not be. In doing so we have allowed ourselves to "settle" for something that's not only less than ideal, but is just flat not necessary and downright harmful and dysfunctional.

COMPASSIONATE NON-ATTACHMENT

Don't get caught up in anyone else's drama or the world's drama. Isn't your plate full enough? How's about you clear your own plate first. Gee, if everyone did this, we'd all have clean plates and the world would be a very different place. So, your fellow human wants to vent and tell you their story, so let 'em. Providing a sounding board is often the very best thing we can do and it's totally effortless. Just listen, don't attach to their drama or enable their continued dysfunction with equally dramatic "sympathy", giving them the standard conditioned, "Ohhh" sob, sob, crinkled-forehead reaction. That does not serve them, you or the world. Practice compassionate non-attachment. Listen, maybe even offer another perspective, but don't dump energy into their drama.

I've listened with compassionate non-attachment to folks who most certainly have experienced the opposite through their lives. As they have related their stories of life experiences to others, the others get so emotionally attached. When they see that I don't get attached, don't show pity or sorrow, but instead listen quietly, with no expression and offer them a different perspective, different way of responding to their situation, they can't help but notice the difference. I've been thanked by folks for "not putting energy into their crap." It doesn't serve either myself or them to do so. When shown something different, they can't help but appreciate it. It gave them a release of the old instead of putting more energy into it. Their vent was then truly a vent.

Here, again, I have to emphasize the energetic level. You could comment on their situation or offer a different perspective and yet go about it with two different energies. In one case, you could be caught up, and, in the other case, you could maintain non-attachment. In both cases, you may very well be using the same words and yet you're bringing a different energy. Even folks who don't understand energy well still can pick up on it at some level.

I saw a post online at Craig's List one day that said this:

"I don't know how to talk to women, because we have all been hurt and are scared to trust that someone is truly interested in making us happy. Craigslist doesn't seem to be the way, but I don't know what else to do??? Any suggestions for showing someone how to be loved and make them comfortable being themselves?"

I responded with this:

"Not something you can MAKE them do. Yep, we're all wounded and we're also being offered a grand opportunity at healing. Some are flowing with that as best they can and others.... not so much. Honey, CL is actually quite representative of people and where they're at right now - like it or lump it. Someone has to love themselves before they can let others love them and before they can love someone else without playing the victim / blame game. If you don't sense that someone wants to move forward (don't have to walk on water, just willing to do the work of healing) then just be thankful you dodged that bullet and LOOK OUT FOR YOURSELF. You are responsible for you and you alone. You cannot do someone else's work for them and you cannot help those who won't be helped. If they won't let you pull them up, at least don't let them pull you down. You have to understand also that all these wounds go back further than a romantic relationship. Our wounds are often activated in childhood. What personal wound could you stand to tend to that makes you want to fix everyone else? Tend to your own back yard. Encourage others to do the same and maybe, just maybe, we all might get out of this self-created pit of hell."

I'll take this opportunity to share some information concerning our human wounds.

A good book that talks about how our body style and posture communicates to us the wounds we came to experience in this lifetime, that we have experienced early in life, that we still carry with us, is Lise Bourbeau's book *Heal Your Wounds and Find Your True Self*. The body doesn't lie. Even when our egos, minds, emotions can tell us one dramatic line of bull, the body only displays our present personal energy.

I've learned how to read faces. Thank you Jean Haner. Here, again, the body is displaying the energy of the personality. The body is the physical manifestation of the personality. A great book on face reading is *Face Reading in Chinese Medicine* by Lillian Bridges. Jean Haner has now turned out her own book also, *The Wisdom of Your Face,* which makes for a great supplement to Lillian's book. Jean and Lillian have worked together also although they have had their own separate paths to this information. Much can be learned about self and others by learning face reading, not the least of which is to remind us that we are not all exactly the same. Knowing one's personality traits can help you work with them. It can help you to understand yourself and others and to accept both. Your own face can give you feedback about changes you're making in your personality and it can also tell you about your health and affected organs so you can then monitor your progress. This understanding tool helps you to step out of judgment.

If your fellow human doesn't give you enough practice at compassionate non-attachment, you can always practice on yourself. Again, it starts with self. Show yourself compassion and do your best to not get caught up even in your own drama. As Shakespear said, "Life is a game, are you playing?"

And world drama? Oh my. So many folks are so caught up. I met a fellow online once. Early in our e-mail conversation, he'd asked me if I had seen the news. I told him I didn't often watch the news. He asked me how could I live without the news. I told him, "Quite happily, thank you." A friend of mine doesn't watch the news either. Someone she works with asked if she had seen a news story. She told them she didn't watch the news. They said, "Well, no wonder you're so up all the time."

Choose wisely where you put your energy and what other energy you allow in. Is the information you take in and the company you keep in line with the path you want to now travel? If you are tired of some aspect of life, why do you continue to immerse yourself in it? Don't put energy into the very thing you don't want to see in this world.

WORD WORKING

Some would say that Jesus H. Christ was a *word*-worker, not a wood-worker. Those two things may very well be very closely related though, as William Henry shows us through the Language of the Birds. It's the Word helping to usher in a new awareness of Wood, or the Quintessence. Let's move forward by moving back to word origins, the true vibration of words. Here are just a few examples.

TERRA / TARA & THE HOMELAND

For some examples of word working used in a manipulative manner, we can first look at George W. Bush's first State of the Union address on September 22, 2001, directly on the heels of 9/11. In his address, Dubya kept referring to the "war on terra / tara", not terror. He said this repeatedly. At one point, he said "murder" and put heavy emphasis on that last 'r'. He did not say "murda." He absolutely knew what he was saying. Terra is, of course, Mother Earth. Tara is peace. He said he'd make war on Earth and Peace. It's said that there was more ecological damage during his term in office than any time prior, and I probably don't need to tell you that he made war on peace.

Many wanted to paint Dubya as a bumbling idiot who kept misspeaking. It's not misspeaking when he meant to say what he did. At one point, he said something to the effect of, "We're restoring chaos as quickly as we can." At another point, he said something to the effect of "They (terrorists) want to take your rights and freedoms away... and so do we." Do not think he was misspeaking. He absolutely knew what he was saying. The Patriot

Act, in supposed response to 9/11, is one big violation of constitutional rights. And don't think that Dubya and those around him during his term in office were the only ones responsible for that act. It was many years in the works, predating Dubya's time in office. It was bipartisan in nature, and those we see in office are just figureheads, front men.

Republicans utilize masculine energy and Democrats utilize feminine energy. Neither masculine or feminine energy, nor anything in this world, is inherently evil, but depends on the intent behind it. The two parties use these energies in negative, controlling ways. Democrats use feminine energy to work in a covert / manipulative way and Republicans use masculine energy to work in an overt / in-yer-face sort of way. Dubya epitomized this. He'd say what their plans were, people would think he misspoke, then he and those he served (no that wouldn't be those that supposedly elected him) would go about doing exactly what he'd said.

Michael Tsarion talks about how Queen Elizabeth's court astrologist, Sir John Dee, made a deal with some other dimensional entities to get some information from them. They told him that they would need human "sacrifices" (perhaps literally, but also just by abuse / control), but there were rules to this game and the victims / sacrifices would have to be warned first. "They", the establishment, continue to do this to this day. They tell us what they are going to do then do it, albeit many times in symbolic ways that the mass of people have forgotten the meaning of, at least at a conscious level, but on other levels these symbols do have meaning and we are then manipulated by them.

Another thing that came up in Dubya's State of the Union address was the first public mention of Homeland Security. This idea of calling the United States "the homeland" just didn't resonate with me. I thought to look up "homeland" in *The Encyclopedic Psychic Dictionary* by June G. Bletzer, Ph. D. I found that homeland refers to the etheric world. So, is it us that "they" are attempting to secure the homeland from?

I obviously wasn't the only one to make this observation. A Twilight Zone episode put out in 2002, that I just happened to catch (synchronistically), called *Chosen,* starring Jake Busey, told the story of some "missionaries" who came to town to ask economically affected citizens to come with them since the end was near. They give the people videos to watch and knew without asking if they needed DVDs or VHS tapes. The missionaries end up being either angels or aliens who grow glowing wings and then take away those who meet with them at the appointed time and location. Jake Busey's character doesn't trust them and doesn't go. After the others are taken away, Homeland Security shows up and is very interested in these "missionaries." They tell Busey to let them know if they show up again. Then the world nuclear holocaust starts. Game over. I found it interesting that in this Twilight Zone story Homeland Security was interested in these beings that may very well have been from the Homeland / etheric world.

OBLIGATION

Oblige

> *Middle English, from Anglo-French obliger, from Latin obligare, literally, to bind to, from ob ' toward' + ligare 'to bind'*

Ah, yes, the ties that bind. Haven't many humans down through the ages worked to not be in bondage, and yet people turn around and willingly hold their wrists out waiting for the cuffs? Doing something out of obligation is quite frankly a crappy reason to be doing it. One could stand to just flat choose to do it or not. But obligation inserts a "have to" into the equation. That in itself is so binding. I certainly don't want anyone agreeing to participate in something with me out of obligation. If they don't really want to do so, and yet do it anyway, they'll bring along a whole lot of less-than-desirable-energy that I could live without, quite frankly.

COMPETITION

Enough with competition already. Well, that is, competition in the modern sense of the word, which usually fits with this definition from Webster:

> *be in a state of rivalry, (and that being):*

> *one of two or more striving to reach or obtain something that only one can possess*

Only one can possess? Why only one? Here's that "either / or" hogwash again. Why does one person striving for something mean the next can't have it also? Goodness sakes.

For many people in today's world, competition falls into the realm of cutting off one's own nose to spite their face. Employers, managers, owners can't seem to stand it that their workers are happy and successful. Their own workers. Hello! The worker's success is the boss's success. There's such a need to keep one's thumb down on someone else they will literally shoot themselves in the foot to keep their workers from being happy and successful.

Romantic partnerships are right there too. Here's the person that one calls the light of their life and yet danged if some people will actually give their partner a hand up. I've experienced partners competing (in the modern sense) in career fields to keep from being the one to stay home to raise the kids not born yet. I've experienced partners not giving constructive feedback, even when asked. I knew it was on their mind since they aired it elsewhere but danged if they'd tell me because they knew I'd capitalize on it. I might have learned something quicker, grown faster and more profoundly if given that feedback. Some people don't seem to want to see someone grow and evolve even when that's someone they love and who would be happy to help pull them up also.

I've played a lot of softball over the years and one could say that sports are about competition, but most of the one-upping going on seems to be between supposed teammates. Enough already! How many tons of bricks does one need to be buried in before we start working together to achieve more than we can separately?

Now, get back to the true vibration of that word and I'm all over that. Dos dictionary informs me that the word origin of compete is from:

Late Latin competere to seek together, from Latin, to come together, agree, be suitable, from com- + petere to go to, seek... com- 'together' + petere 'aim at, seek'

Aim at or seek together. Let's go there already!

COMPATIBLE

The true vibration of this word would have a connotation that many today would judge to be "negative."

Late middle English: from French, from medieval Latin compatiblis, from compati 'suffer with'

Literally "able to suffer with." I don't see this as a "negative" thing at all. Now, of course, we will draw others to us that have similar issues to work on, or who have complementary issues that, in turn, provide a reflection, mirroring our issues to us. This is an opportunity, not a crisis.

I worked with an astrologer for years who told me this story. She would get together with other astrologers to compare notes. They would look at charts of famous people. They looked at Angelina Jolie and Billy Bob Thornton when those two had first gotten together. All the other astrologers thought they were a "match made in Heaven". My astrologer sat there and shook her head. They asked why. She told them there was not enough challenge between their charts and they would get bored with each other and, sure enough, they split up six months later.

Yes, indeed, compatible. The "head knocking" and the "suffering" parts of a relationship provide the lessons, the growth opportunities, the opportunity to awaken. Of course, the so-called "good" stuff has to be there to balance it, at least enough to make us stick around long enough to get the lesson.

Instead of those folks who make mountains out of molehills and head for the hills at the first sign of work, I like to see the kind of folks who work over the speed bumps with me. Quite frankly, I love to have folks in my life who are "able to suffer with" me... and in the end, still be there, long after the experience of suffering is gone. Sign me up!

"NO" IS A PERFECTLY ACCEPTABLE ANSWER.

Many people have great difficulty with this concept that "no" is a perfectly acceptable answer. The conditioning and wounds surrounding the word "no" are very deeply ingrained. People have been conditioned to think that telling someone "no" is somehow bad or inconsiderate or selfish. It's as if that word is evil. This happens on both transmit and receive.

I can't count the times I've set boundaries with people and had to say "no" to something, then watched the ensuing temper tantrum, out of supposed adults. They will scratch and claw and hold on for dear life to something that was never theirs in the first place. It's like the old line, "What part of 'no' don't you understand?"

I've dealt with people who won't take no for an answer, so they push and push to get what they want. I have to get a little firmer, maybe a little louder with my no, then they accuse me of having a temper. Well, date rapists don't take no for an answer either. Does that mean that when the woman finally kicks and scratches and claws to get them off of her that she has a temper? Nothing quite like shifting the responsibility.

And it's oh so fun to turn from saint to the spawn of Satan in these folks' minds... all because they don't want to hear "no". Not that the person who said "no" has changed in any way. Interestingly enough, and as these things go in this human / earthly experience, many of the people who resist a "no" answer the hardest are those who have had their own boundaries violated. Many were subjected to abuse of various sorts as part of their childhood experience, and yet they turn right around and show disrespect for the next person's boundaries, as if they have some "entitlement" to others' lives, emotions, thoughts and physicality. They have the mentality of they WILL have their way, perhaps because someone had their way with them when they were children. And the cycle of abuse continues. Might I take this opportunity to say that the Golden Rule is still one of the simplest and yet most profound bits of wisdom there is. If you don't want to see something in this world, then don't put energy into it yourself - at any level!

And getting a "no" answer out of someone seems just as challenging. I once asked someone if they could help me with something. I gave them all the details upfront so there would be and were no surprises later on. Initially, they were very emphatically affirming they would help, but then came the waffling. I've gotten trained by such folks to hear the "no" that they really mean and yet can't seem to bring themselves to say as they squirm this way and that to get out of their initial "yes". Wouldn't it have all been much simpler to just say "no"... at any time during this whole process? And these folks seem to think that leaving someone hanging or saying they'll do something they've no intention of doing is somehow less harmful than just saying no. Then when I let them know I was covered and had found someone else to help out, I then got the dramatic extended ramble of their guilt trip. What is there to feel guilty about? Just say "no" already. I told them I had no problem with the fact that they could not help, but just needed a straight, honest answer so I could then find someone who could help. In being honest with themselves and others by just saying no, they not only serve their needs, they are serving those others also by not leaving them hanging or letting them down.

Then there are those who go ahead and say "no," but then feel they have to justify why they said "no". I injured myself once and was looking for someone to help me with a few things that I couldn't do on my own and needed to be addressed in the near future. I called someone and asked them. They said, "I can't." Well, I have no problem accepting "no" for an answer so I said, "Ok. Thanks. Goodbye," and disconnected. I get a call back immediately and this person wants to tell me all their life drama. Here I was in a rare position of needing some help and was tired and in pain. I'm very self sufficient usually, but not so independent and prideful to not ask for help when I could use it. And I was doing just that and yet even when I'm tired and in pain this person wants to tell me their life drama. It's like yelling out the window of a burning building to someone to help you and they say, "Nope, can't help you 'cause I'm stewing on my divorce and I want to tell you all about it and you'd better be quiet and listen up, so don't even think about yelling out to the next person on the street who could help you out of that burning building."

And this same person was so very focused on their own self-made drama and saw so many things as negative. Even life sending help and blessings they viewed as negative. Prior to this, I'd offered help to them on things and they would not accept my help. They very begrudgingly were accepting help from someone else who was basically putting a roof over their head and yet they still managed to make this help sound like torture in some way. As opposed to not having a roof over their head? And the person providing the roof was not abusing them in any way, just helping them out. This acquaintance had dug themselves a very deep hole by spending decades of worrying about how they could help other people. They'd expended so much energy their whole life worrying about others that when the actual opportunity arose for them to help someone, they were too deep in their own burnout to lend a hand and then wouldn't let me go to find someone who could help me. It was well within their capability to help me do a few little things. What they were going on about I could not help with and they would not have accepted my help if there was something I could do and, like I said, I had offered with what was in my ability to do.

The reason behind a "no" answer is really of no consequence. The answer is still no. I've had people take a romantic interest in me when I don't return it. They'll ask why. Why ask why? Just what do they plan on doing with that information? What? Are they going to change for me? That's not a good reason to change. If they were fine with who they are, then it would serve them to be who they are. If they change for someone else, then it's false change and will eventually come back and bite them and those involved with them. Are they going to use the information to get into an argument with me to justify who they are? I never told them they couldn't be who they are, I just said I wasn't interested in romantic involvement with them. Period. End of discussion. Not really something you'd want to twist someone's arm about, well, unless you just can't get enough drama.

I've also experienced folks who make a commitment, say, to have dinner with me. When the time came, what they really could have used more than going out to dinner with me was some time alone to rest and relax, but they felt so obligated to stick to the dinner date that they brought their burnt-out, grumpy self to share with me at dinner. I think I would have much rather received a call saying they couldn't make it. Not only did it not serve them to not say "no", they weren't doing me any favors either. Seems rather pointless. We'd arranged to see each other to enjoy each other's company. How enjoyable is the company of someone frazzled, tired or hurried?

And for those that actually do say no, I can't help but thank them for saying so and if it's because they need to take care of themselves first, you can bet that I applaud them for that also. Ah, how refreshing – someone who has their priorities straight.

"No" and "stop" are not dirty words. I'll repeat again, "no" is a perfectly acceptable answer. Learn to say it. Learn to accept it. Respect people's boundaries, your own included, most especially your own. Don't be scared to communicate your boundaries. And keep in mind that there are many ways to communicate. If someone is doing something that is over your boundary line and yet you don't say or do anything to communicate that to them or otherwise make it stop, how will they know? Not saying or doing anything IS communicating something. It communicates that what they are doing is ok. If it's not ok, then make sure they know that, then do what you need to do to look out for yourself.

THE HUMAN MIND DOES NOT REGISTER NEGATION.

Now, I'll have to talk about another angle of "no". Hopefully you'll see the difference between this and the previous section (although this may explain why some folks just can't take no for an answer, lol).

I found this explanation online of negation in terms of language: "Negation is a morphosyntactic operation in which a lexical item denies or inverts the meaning of another lexical item or construction. A negator is a lexical item that expresses negation. Examples: not, non-, un-."

Boy, don't you wish you could get paid for all those $10 grammatical terms?!

If I told you "don't think about monkeys", well, gee, what are you thinking about now? Could it possibly be "monkeys"? Your thoughts and energy are now on monkeys. Well, that's not so bad, eh. Monkeys are kinda cute. Now, if our speed of manifestation were instant, we could perhaps find ourselves buried in monkeys every time someone told us to not think about monkeys. Our present speed of creation is not instantaneous, but, as we increase the frequency of our vibrational energy, we are manifesting more and more quickly. We are constantly creating.

The human mind does not register negation, but it most certainly registers that thing that we are trying to negate, like aforementioned monkeys. We all have been so conditioned to express ourselves with negation. When doing so, we are putting energy into the very thing that we would rather not see in the world. Mother Teresa was once asked if she would march against war. She said she would not march "against" anything, but, if they wanted to have a march FOR peace, she would be there.

What do the following phrases make you think of and direct your energy towards?

Just say no to drugs. No Iraq War. Stop teen violence.

... and all the endless signs with the red circle and diagonal line through it with the word or picture in the middle standing out larger than life. What about all the endless "ribbon" stickers on backs of cars reminding you of war or "don't forget to get your breast cancer!" etc. Weapons are not allowed in schools. Duh. And yet outside the schools now are signs saying no weapons. They might as well put up a sign that says, "Don't forget your weapons... and your tobacco too, don't forget that. We'll keep reminding you." Energy flows where attention goes. What we resist persists. One website I saw of some folks that were attempting to awaken people to some of what truly goes on in this world, unfortunately, had this on their site: "Resist the flood of ignorance." Makes me wonder how much ignorance they are attracting their way with that one. I'll bet it wouldn't take much to express that in more positive terms that don't put the focus on ignorance.

And then there's all those endless AA and NA meetings. So instead of drinking and drugging, we'll just all sit around and talk about not drinking and drugging. What's wrong with that picture? We may as well all sit around and talk about not thinking about monkeys.

I found this online (at www.worldtrans.org):

There is no such thing as "No __(Something)__ " in the real world. It is purely a construct of the mind. You won't be able to find ideas like "No respect", "No trust", "No luck" anywhere but in somebody's mind. You won't be able to actually observe the lack of any beingness, doingness, or havingness around you. There are all kinds of things one can observe in the world. Not one of them is a negative. The world is full of things that are there. Ideas about what *ought to be there, but isn't, relate to people's mental and emotional responses to what IS there. Negation is also just a mental construct. And one that only seems to make any sense for the conscious portion of the person. **The sub-conscious ignores negation.** (my emphasis)*

As we'll see later in the section Our Beliefs as Our Environment, that last sentence is highly significant. Our subconscious is usually running the show as it takes care of those "automatic" learned things. So, yeah, our minds don't register the negation... just the monkeys.

And look at all of us talking about not negating something. My god. If two wrongs don't make a right, then how many negations of things that don't exist will make any of it actually exist or not? Mind-boggling isn't it? That same article encourages that we convert negatives to positives when we can. Indeed. Perhaps one day we'll have negated all the negations to the point where we won't even have any idea of the concept of negating anything. Such concepts will be unfathomable.

And yet we're not quite there yet. In order to communicate, we're still at the stage of having to use some negation to some degree. Eckhart Tolle speaks of similar. He talks of how we will eventually get to a point where we will be communicating without words. He refers to the *Course in Miracles*, which teaches just this. And yet they use a whole lot of words to get you there. As Eckhart states, the *Course in Miracles* meets you where you are and takes you to a new place. Again, this prioritizes things, puts things in the right order. You can't take a society of people who are used to communicating through words and negations and have them suddenly drop those forms of communication. Just like the rest of life, communication is a process, but we can consciously clean up our language and express things in positive terms as much as possible. We can insist on peace instead of negating its negative.

And on that note, I'll be using negation now...

STOP THE CYCLE OF ABUSE

As I mentioned earlier, if there is something you don't want to see in the world, don't put energy into it. In this last age, the Age of Pisces, we've been intensely conditioned to tap into the "down" side

66

of Pisces. We all have the martyr / victim / blame game down. Pain and Suffering has been a great teacher, but we must finally learn the lessons from our old teacher so we can advance to the next grade, to go on to a new age and a new teacher. In the Age of Aquarius, that teacher will be Discovery, which sounds like a whole lot more fun than that old battle axe, Pain and Suffering.

This is an experiential realm. We contract with other souls, especially early in life, to have wounds activated so we can experience that. The wounds taint and skew our lives and, in a defensive mode or for desire of love or attention, we often compromise our true selves almost out of existence. We move further and further away from ourselves until it becomes unbearable, too painful to continue down that path. In order to go on, we must make changes.

Until we make that turnaround, we all too often continue to dump energy into the cycle of ab-use. Someone feels they were ab-used earlier in life by parents, siblings, other family members, preachers, teachers, peers and partners. The wounds are deep. The anger, frustration and pain are intense. People continue through their lives willingly playing the victim because of old wounds, but for this drama to be complete, they need a villain. So they recruit whoever stands before them to play that role of villain so they can, in turn, be the victim. They take out their pent up emotions on the person who stands before them, who was not on the scene when their wounds were activated, not even as a witness to the original ab-use. The "victim" becomes suspicious of everyone, trusting no one. In their victim way of being, they are passing on the woundedness and ab-using others.

Norah Jones covered the Hank Williams song, *Cold Cold Heart,* which sums up this scenario in the romantic realm quite nicely:

> *I've tried so hard, my dear, to show that you're my every dream*
> *Yet you're afraid each thing I do is just some evil scheme*
> *A memory from your lonesome past keeps us so far apart*
> *Why can't I free your doubtful mind and melt your cold cold heart?*

67

Another love before my time made your heart sad and blue
And so my heart is payin' now for things I didn't do
In anger, unkind words I say that make the teardrops start
Why can't I free your doubtful mind and melt your cold cold heart?

There was a time where I believed that you belonged to me
But now I know your heart is shackled to a memory
The more I learn to care for you, the more we drift apart
Why can't I free your doubtful mind and melt your cold cold heart?

If you find yourself playing the victim and passing on your woundedness to the next person who had no part in your wounding, catch yourself and refuse to continue the cycle of ab-use. If you don't like it done to you, then don't do it to the next person. Don't put energy into the very thing you don't like to see in the world.

And if you find someone attempting to cast you in the role of villain, refuse to accept the role. Say "no", put your foot down, and don't put energy into their victim / blame game. Don't enable their dysfunction. If necessary, move away from their drama.

Like I said before, there are many ways to communicate. If someone is being ab-usive and you say or do nothing to make it stop, you're still communicating. And what you're communicating through your lack of action or lack of vocalizing is that what they are doing is ok. It's not ok. Don't let yourself think so. Don't let them think so either. If you truly care about this person who is ab-using you, who is unconsciously attempting to pass on their woundedness to you, do whatever is necessary to make it clear to them that their ab-use is not acceptable. If you have to leave their lives to hammer home the message, then do so. Be courageous enough to show them the love and compassion involved in NOT enabling their continued dysfunction.

Some of you may remember comedienne Brett Butler, who was very popular a few years back. She also had her own sitcom called *Grace Under Fire*. In her sitcom, she had a character who was her own character's abusive ex-husband. This paralleled her own life. Over several years, she put out the story of her ex who used to hit her. Well, a few years into her popularity, I saw her perform her standup routine. In the middle of it, she got rather sober and serious for a bit. She spoke of this past relationship with her ex-husband, but in a very different light than how I'd heard her speak of it before. She had come to realize, and was there to share with us, her role in that interaction. She was there to shoulder the responsibility of that role she has played. She said that she and her ex would get into arguments and she would very intentionally egg him on in an effort to get to his breaking point and get him to hit her. If he did, then she felt in that moment that she had "won." In the theater that day, she fessed up to how abusive HER actions were. She confessed her "sin" before her audience, courageous soul that she is. I understand how her ex husband felt. I've been the one who's been egged on. Being subjected to such passive-aggressive abuse is not a fun thing to experience.

Many have gotten to where they think that physical abuse is the only kind there is, or that it is somehow worse than any other. Keep in mind, there are many forms of ab-use and none are more acceptable than another. People are doling out passive-aggressive, mind screwing abuses and there is often no one offering to come to the abused's assistance in those cases. And then when the abused has finally had enough and defends themselves, they are the ones painted as the abuser. Stories of this nature offer examples of not just how brainwashed and dysfunctional the individuals involved are, but also our whole society. The onlookers who would step right in if someone were beating on someone will let the passive-aggressive abuse just go on.

I caught a Dr. Phil one day about this controlling, passive-aggressive type of thing. A husband was very controlling of his wife. He had hidden a GPS tracking device in her car and sat at his computer and monitored her whereabouts when she left. He had hidden cameras all around the house. She couldn't go anywhere or do anything without his permission and oftentimes was forced to stay home. He was starting to really isolate her from other people. While on the Dr. Phil show, he claimed he would never hit her or hurt her. Dr. Phil said that was a compound sentence and, even though he was not hitting her, he was still hurting her. Thank God this fellow had agreed to be on the show and they got some help. I say this because, especially in a situation where someone becomes isolated, they end up with no one to turn to, no one to believe that there is such ab-use going on. And even if surrounded by friends, due to societal conditioning, many people would not see this sort of thing for the ab-use that it truly is.

Passive-aggressive behavior can present itself in very subtle ways. And, one more time, the subtle is very powerful. Passive-aggressive types may do something as simple as always being late. That puts them in control of the situation. I've dealt with people like this before myself. Being late was the rule and not the exception with them. On the few rare occasions that I would be late, they'd go through the roof. One thing that whole situation taught me was to no longer wait on anyone. If they're late for dinner, then they'll eat dinner late. It doesn't mean I have to. I wasn't late, they were. They can face the consequences of their own actions by themselves. It's their ride and I don't have to go on it with them. With the folks who do have some issues and yet still have a little going for them, when I quit waiting for them, they got the message and their being late habit stopped. The dysfunctional part of themselves couldn't seem to get that message by discussing it with them over and over, and yet just not waiting for them hammered it home.

The Dr. Phil story speaks of control of someone in an overall sense, controlling someone's every move, knowing their whereabouts, etc. Jealousy and possessiveness represent a subset of that. It's about treating someone as a piece of property instead of respecting them as a human being with the right of Free Will, with every right to have whatever experiences they choose to have. Keep in mind that the "victim" of control is playing a vital role in this. If you allow yourself to be controlled, you are giving authority of your life away. No one can truly take authority over us, but we most certainly can give it away. And not only does it not serve us, it also does not serve the other. Like I talked about before, if you do or say nothing to stop someone from doing something, you're still communicating something - that their behavior is ok. Jealousy and possessiveness are not ok. They're dysfunctional. By allowing yourself to be controlled by another, you're enabling their continued dysfunction. You're giving them no constructive feedback to tell them they could stand to shed that issue. You're just reinforcing their issue, helping them justify their own dysfunction. Is that the loving thing to do? You are, in effect, helping them NOT heal.

I heard a TV evangelist speak on such things. He was talking about money and attracting it into your life, but his wisdom could apply to other areas also. He said that a best friend will tell you what you're doing right. A mentor will tell you what you're doing wrong. A best friend wants your approval. A mentor wants you to succeed. Sometimes if we really want to do what's best for someone, we have to give them some tough love, we have to be brave enough to tell it like it is and back those words up with action, if necessary.

Sometimes all the situation calls for is to allow others a release, a vent. But, at the same time, it's still about not enabling their dysfunction, about not engaging in their drama with them. I read a book a while back called *Relationships: Gifts of the Spirit* by Julie Hutslar. In one section, Julie speaks of something she learned from a healer named Gabrell. He told her that sometimes when dealing with our loved ones we have to "dodge the arrows." He told her that when she runs into her husband's triggers and he goes off on her to just stand there and radiate love towards him and let the arrows fly by since they really aren't meant for her anyway. She expressed that would be a very challenging thing to do. He said, "Yeah, you're gonna get some on ya."

Well, I was in a romantic relationship with someone a while back. We were not involved for very long. From the first time we met to the last time we saw each other was only three months. Their favorite way of dealing with issues as they came up was to not deal. I often joked that I saw an awful lot of their ass and elbows as they kept running away every time there was a bump in the road. We had a strong energetic connection and, as these things go, that often means, bare minimum, that there are major growth opportunities being offered. I knew going into it, it was not something that would last, but Life laid out the red carpet and said, "Go here." This was an experience that I was to have.

Afterward, I certainly had no regrets. I was being offered tests on lessons previously learned and the opportunities to clear and release old wounds and issues. I was to be myself and do what I

71

knew was right regardless of the arrows slung from my severely wounded fellow human. When this person was in their more lucid moments, they absolutely knew what their triggers were about, but, when the next trigger came, it was like flipping a switch and they were back in their childhood wounds full force. I too was having my triggers tweaked, but could catch myself on it in the moment and make a course correction in short order. But when I did go off just a bit at the start, that seemed to signal to this person to engage with me. They cut me no slack, even though I was handling my triggers far better than they were theirs. I had them read the "Gabrell's Open Heart" section of Julie Hutslar's book. I asked if they could do their best to let my arrows go by for the brief time it took me to catch myself. They understood, but, in the time we were together, I did not witness them being able to dodge my arrows.

One day we went out for lunch. I came to realize later that they interpreted the words "no" and "stop" as yelling. They had heard many arguments between their parents as a child and this was one of their triggers. Later, in their lucid moments, they spoke of accusing people their whole lives of yelling at them or being mad at them when that was not the case. And as with me, the others' reassurances made no difference when they were in "trigger" mode. Well, that day I had told them to stop in reference to getting a parking spot that was opening up. Little did I know at the time that I had just run into a big trigger. I got the, "stop yelling at me" gig and lunch was not a pleasant experience.

We got done with lunch and were walking down the street. Our conversation was not very fruitful at pulling them out of their trigger mode. Through all of this, I kept thinking about Gabrell's open heart and dodging the arrows that I knew were not for me. It was a nice day and I had my jacket hanging over my shoulder. Suddenly, a dive-bombing bird hit his target - my shoulder! Luckily it was the one with the jacket over it. I busted up laughing, realizing I had just "got some on me." The Divine certainly has a sense of humor. I can't imagine what sort of fireworks it would have set off for the person I was with if it had been them that received the bomb hit, but, for me, it was just the Divine reminding me to keep dodging the arrows and have some fun with all this, even if the other person couldn't muster that.

A friend of mine says, "Remember the rule - only one crazy person at a time." There's been plenty of times when I wondered when I was going to get to be the crazy one, ya know, by myself, without the other engaging with me. In relation to this, despair.com strikes again, *"Please remain calm. It's no use us both being hysterical at the same time."*

The second of The Four Agreements from Don Miguel Ruiz (www.miguelruiz.com) states:

2. Don't Take Anything Personally

Nothing others do is because of you. What others say and do is a projection of their own reality, their own dream. When you are immune to the opinions and actions of others, you won't be the victim of needless suffering.

Reminds me of the line, "What you think of me is none of my business." This requires we hone our discernment to tell when we are getting a Divine message through other people or when we are only seeing their projection onto us. Ask, "What's in this for me?" If this is not your lesson, then your role may be as the messenger, the catalyst or the teacher role for another. Perhaps the biggest part of the lesson is there for the other. That "What's in this for me?" question only goes so far. We can ask ourselves why someone's actions or words bother us and we may very well find our own buttons / triggers behind that. But it may be a case of perhaps what's in it for you is the opportunity to put your foot down, to stick up for yourself, to say, "Enough already!" and do what it takes to end what is in reality an abusive situation.

A friend of mine was telling me about things that her husband does that he consciously knows bothers her and, in turn, will set up a situation that really is not fun for him either. Perhaps just like an addict, he gets something from the resulting interaction. Perhaps an argument that follows is an adrenaline rush for him. He repeatedly insists on this behavior when at any other level than getting some rush out of it, he really has no reason to do this, even for his sake. My friend said she could stand to ask herself why it bothers her. Indeed. It's useful for that to be the first question. But, like I said, this only goes so far. If you were to make the analogy of someone out of the blue punching you in the nose every day and then ask,

"Well why does this bother me?" well, that makes it rather clear, eh? It's abusive. That's why it bothers you.

So, here again, we have to strike a balance. What part of this drama is mine, what part is the other's? This is key, for we can only work on our side of it. We can only change ourselves and our reaction to people or situations. We cannot do another's work for them. But, as our frequency changes, that affects the frequency of those around us, well, if you can hang in there long enough for them to shift. If their shift doesn't happen quickly enough, you need not leave yourself to dodging arrows on their target range forever. Those arrows aren't meant for you anyway and you can still love this person unconditionally from afar, if need be.

THE FOUR SIDES OF THE PYRAMID

In William Henry's video presentation of *Starwalkers and the Dimension of the Blessed*, he speaks of the four Greek words for the different kinds of Love. He leads into this with a depiction from a Tarot deck of pyramid builders. A pyramid must be built up equally on all sides or it will topple. The pyramid has four sides representing physical, mental, emotional, and spiritual parts of ourselves. If we don't tend to all of these, our pyramid will be out of balance.

He goes on to say that we can also get out of balance with expressing the four different kinds of love. Here are the four Greek words for the different kinds of Love:

Eros - sexual, erotic or romantic love.

Storge - family love, the kind of love there is between parent and child or towards a pet.

Philia - brotherly friendship and affection. It is the love of deep friendship or partnership. It might be described as the highest love of which man, without God's help, is capable.

Agape - compassionate, selfless love directed equally toward all people.

I have witnessed in my own personal interactions with my fellow humans that people can often delude themselves concerning these types of love. Examples of what I mean here are like the person

74

who wants romantic love when all you have to offer them is friendship. I find that many folks only equate the word "love" to romantic love and get very black and white about it. If one or both parties are not interested in romantic love, many people pass up the friendship potential and move on.

One person, who I hoped would be a friend, was obviously looking to me for romance. I made it clear that all I had to offer was friendship. They said they totally understood and yet I could tell by things they'd said and done afterward that they really didn't understand. I clarified even more. This time they did get it and, judging by their response, they had not gotten it after the first time I'd told them. They then said that they would not be putting as much energy into our relationship. I told them it wasn't about how MUCH energy, but what TYPE of energy. We can put a lot of energy into friends, but that doesn't make them lovers. As William Henry speaks about, all of these four kinds of love could stand to be nurtured. Why pass up a potentially good friendship just because there's no hope of romance? We're cheating ourselves by doing so.

And telling someone you love them when you mean in an agape / universal way really trumps a lot of folks up. A friend of mine says she'll tell folks she loves them and clarifies with, "... but we won't be picking out curtains together." Others keep investing romantic love energy into someone who will not return it, dumping energy down a dead end street. This "ties up" their eros energy in a place that it will not fruit. It doesn't serve anyone involved.

I've been in long-term relationships where the romantic eros energy was there originally, but obviously dwindled for my partner. I told them that if they were no longer interested in me in that way that was fine. That's perfectly acceptable. It's certainly not anything to be argued. But I had to ask them, "If that's the case, why are you still here?" Like Melissa Etheridge's lyrics, *"If you can't love me then let me go."* Or as the Supremes sang,

> *"Set me free why doncha babe*
> *Let me be why doncha babe*
> *Cuz you don't really love me,*
> *you just keep me hangin' on"*

This partner kept telling me "I'm trying." Try implies past and present failure. Every time we say "try" we may as well finish with "... and fail." I can't help but think that even those who are not consciously aware of the meaning of "try" still do understand it at some level. Implications being that they really don't want that person, job, situation, etc., that they keep "trying" so hard for.

"Do or do not. There is no try." Yoda

Not only does it not serve us to invest romantic energy into someone who won't return it, it also doesn't serve either party to act as if it's still there for us when it's not. The type of love energy may shift. Perhaps you'll go from being romantic lovers to being friends, but be kind to both people involved and don't put out the message to the world of "lover" energy when it's really now a friendship. Don't tie up your own or your now friend's romantic eros energy. Energetically release both of you. Cut that cord.

And even those folks who are not consciously aware of people's energy still pick up on it unconsciously. We are all better at reading each other than we care to admit to and we'll read ourselves and others much better if we "get out of our own way" and stop deluding ourselves. Be honest with yourself first so you can be honest with the people around you and honor their wishes. You can't change them. You never will. What you can do is change how you handle the situations and people that are presented to you. It's your response to Life that you have anything resembling control over. Be responsible, as in able to respond.

Perhaps we'd all be better off if we re-adopted using four words to describe these types of love rather than just one. Just that alone may help the whole world adjust their attitudes about the various kinds of relationship. The old way of thinking about "love" even affects those folks outside a relationship, the people around two people having the relationship.

Here are some examples from my personal life on such things. One long-term ex and I, when we split up, learned how our friends had put our relationship on a pedestal. Almost all our friends scattered to the winds. My ex had maintained contact with one couple and I maintained contact with a couple people. We both attempted to maintain contact with others to no avail. Those that did stay in our lives gave us some clue as to why that was. My ex's friend said, "If you two can't make it, who can?" My friend said, "I still don't understand why you two split up." Like we were serving as role models for them. What's sad is that we really were serving as good examples. It's just that how we went about that did not fit their delusional expectations. My ex and I were friends after we split up. Our relationship shifted to something different. The romantic partner gig no longer worked for us, but we did love and respect each other and appreciated each other, but not being involved romantically didn't seem to fit our friends' expectations for us.

After our split up, this same ex realized early on not to refer to me as an ex when introducing me to new people, as they automatically assumed there was bad blood there. In order to keep their baggage off of us, my ex would just introduce me as a friend and that's what we were, never mind that level of friendship was, in part, due to the shared experiences we'd had as partners and understanding of each other's families, history, etc.

Another long-term ex of mine eventually became a good friend of mine. We had some energy to clear, some things to sort out, some growth and healing to go through after our split, which included cleaning up some issues that were making it difficult for us to be friends also, energies that didn't work any better as friends as when we were partners, but we both stepped up. It was a sheer joy to see this ex's growth, usually something I've only been able to see in myself, as many other people come and go and so I don't get to see their growth over time. This ex and I most certainly have had a strong connection. I'm completely convinced at this point that we have been soul mates of sorts, as we have obviously been in each other's lives to help each other in this world, in this lifetime. And yet here, again, some people around us just can't stand to see such a strong connection and yet that connection is of a friend variety. We met someone once that couldn't help but notice our connection and said we were bound to get back together. Good thing we don't have to live up to anyone else's expectations. Here, again, part of why we were so close after shifting to friends is because of many years of shared experiences. We made this shift in relationship energy, regardless of the highly conditioned souls all around us.

If someone truly loves someone unconditionally, they will love them whether the person is in their life or not. I've told people that, like those song lyrics, I loved them before I met them and I love them after they are gone from my life. So very many people still do not understand this concept of unconditional love of an agape sort. There are some folks whose present energy I'd rather not be around, but that doesn't mean I love them any less.

WE ARE WHAT WE DRAW LIFEFORCE FROM

As the old line goes, we are what we eat. In our present human earthly experience we sustain our own lives by taking lifeforce from our food and yet the establishment bamboozled the farmers into using chemical fertilizers that strip minerals out of the soil, to dump pesticides on our foods, and now big seed suppliers like Monsanto, through genetically modified organisms (GMOs), have even put the pesticides right into the genetic makeup of the plants. The food industry refines and processes out further nutrients. Then they might put some of those nutrients back in through "enrichment" and "fortification," but not in the synergistic blend that nature did that is so important for our bodies to properly utilize the nutrients. Often trace minerals are left out. Someone told me once of Adelle Davis being on the Johnny Carson show back in the 70s. She was describing how the food industry was messing with our food and, henceforth, our health. The person telling me this said they had no idea why, but Johnny was really giving her grief over this. At one point he said, "But Adelle, they enrich these processed foods with nutrients." She came back with, "Well, Johnny, if you gave me $20 and I gave you $5 back, would you feel enriched?"

We have even removed our senses from the equation. Raw sugar is brown, refined sugar is white. Whole grain flour is brown, processed flour is white. There is no such thing as white rice, it doesn't grow that way. The nutrients are processed out of brown rice to make rice white. Sweet potatoes are loaded with nutrients, regular potatoes are pretty much mostly just starch. Food is improperly grown, processed, refined. They feel a need to add artificial "flavors" to what's left to even get us to eat it. We're eating so-called food that has no color, no odor, no flavor. What is it that indicates to us that this is food? We have our five senses to be sensible. And yet we ignore our senses, 'cause, hey, the food "experts" must know what they are doing, right?

Oh, yeah, at the top of the food industry, those making the decisions absolutely know what they are doing. Indeed they do.

78

Their agenda is to control and disempower, not to provide good healthy food. I met a gal once that said she tells conventional food eaters that there is no food in their food. Color, odor and flavor indicate what kind of and what level of nutrients are in food. When we deny and defy our first five senses, what chance do we have of tapping into our sixth sense? Cut your body off from crucial nutrients and you're also cutting yourself off from spirit. Our bodies, minds, emotions and spirit are the four sides of a pyramid that is very unstable if we do not build up all equally. Our bodies are antennas, communicators, and life-sustaining vehicles for us here in this realm. Don't take care of your temple and you won't know spirit. Cut off spirit and your emotions are affected. Screw up the chemical balance in our bodies and our minds don't function properly. All parts of us yearn for balance.

Food that has its nutrients stripped out of it and only has the energy part, the carbohydrates in it, has, in effect, been turned into something toxic. The body doesn't have the nutrients necessary to process the carbs. It then stores those carbs in fat, along with other toxins, like pesticides and food additives. Things like aspartame are very toxic and, henceforth, diet pop will put weight on you, not take it off. Not to mention what other ill affects it has on your health.

Maury Povich repeatedly gets extremely obese children and their parents on his show. His angle is total sensationalism. He sits there and makes the parents feel bad for making their kids fat. The parents are NOT malicious, they are just ignorant. Unfortunately, Povich does nothing to educate them. Lord knows if he has a clue himself. They show footage of the kids pounding donuts, processed pasta and the like. The kids keep eating because they are literally starving. If they were fed some real, whole, organic food, their hunger would be satiated from the nutrients in it and they would not only quit eating so much, they'd lose weight, as their bodies now have some nutrients to process all the stored carbs and toxins in their body fat. Our bodies do their best to survive with what we give them. If we load 'em down with toxins, they store it away in fat in hopes that this is a temporary situation. And when fueled properly, our bodies can then undo the damage we've done.

A friend sent me some youtube videos about some folks who did some intentional and in one case unintentional experiments with fast food. Bottom line, some of this food refused to spoil. It's not spoiling because there is nothing, even at the microbial level, that sees it as food. The decomposition bacteria don't even want to eat it. I told my friend that the same is said about gluten. If pure gluten were piled on the ground, it would stay there indefinitely because nothing will eat it. I told her this further supports my suspicion that the powers that be messing with our food supply is not something that's only recent. Our top grains are all gluten grains - wheat, barley, rye - and they have been around for a VERY long time, like since the whole Mesopotamia / cradle of civilization / post deluge time. Wild versions of grains don't have gluten. The entities that genetically manipulated earth humans way back when were quite the genetic engineers and tampered with both plants and animals. Gee, in today's world, here we go again on that ride with the whole GMO thing.

If a main component of these grains, gluten, is one of the top food allergens and even decomposition bacteria won't eat it, what is it that makes us think this is food? I found an article online that spoke of a study of the diet of hunter / gatherers. They ate meat, veggies, fruit, nuts and seeds. They did NOT eat grains.

As I talked about earlier under EITHER / OR VS AND / BOTH, the food industry wants to put the four top food allergens - soy, dairy, gluten and corn - into everything. I've been a wheat and barley farmer's daughter and a beer brewer and yet I'm here to tell you that gluten grains aren't doing any of us any favors, most especially in the quantities we are consuming. Those that have an immune response (and that is what it is) to gluten are really the lucky ones. At least they know they should avoid it. The rest of us are getting poisoned slowly. The ones that are sensitive are the canaries in the coal mine.

Even natural, organic food suppliers and grocers, even though acknowledging dairy and gluten issues, are still stuck on using unfermented soy protein in many deli items or selling prepackaged food containing soy protein. They'll argue the vegetarian / vegan diet. Ok, so you want to be a vegetarian, then eat your veggies for goodness sakes. If you know you can live healthfully without meat, then don't let the food industry talk you into needing a "meat substitute" called soy protein that is slowly depleting your health. If you don't need meat, then why would you need a meat substitute?

We should be able to get enough protein from plant sources anyway.

I've known a few ex-vegetarians. Their health took a nose-dive when on a "vegetarian" diet. They had eaten one hell of a lot of soy. They eventually went back to meat eating and swore off soy. I'm not totally convinced they needed to go back to meat (I think meat eating really is an individual thing, some may need it, some may not), but I am convinced the soy was what did a number on 'em. Soy protein is the toxic waste product of the industrial uses of soy. If the soy industry did not convince people it was food, they would have to pay dearly to dispose of it. Why pay to dispose of it when you can talk humans into buying it and become a living, breathing filter to get rid of your waste through?

As with everything else, the energetic level is subtle and yet significant. Our intent surrounding our food is very significant. It's important that the growing, handling, transporting and preparation of food be done with the proper intent and respect. There's a reason why people bless their meal, but we may have forgotten where to send those blessings - to the food itself. I often send energy back in time to my food and wish it a happy, healthy life.

The "reality" we have known requires we take something else's life to sustain our own life. There are some folks in this world that offer us a glimpse of our potential to be able to sustain our own lifeforce without having to kill something in order to survive ourselves. Breatharians can literally live off of air alone. Some Tibetan Buddhists have been known to live off of sunlight alone.

The way of things here can be equated to school. And this earthly realm is absolutely our classroom in an experiential sense. By the rules of this realm, you don't get to advance to second grade until you've passed first grade. (But "rules" are just part of the illusion of this realm, we'll get to that later.) It might be a nice thought to not have to take the life of something else to live ourselves, but, until we've mastered that, we're still gonna be in first grade. And how will we master this experience of eating other living things? A little honor and respect might help. And here, again, it starts with self. As I said, we are what we eat. Gee, I don't know, are we respecting the plants and animals we raise for food? One look at increasing health issues with humans should answer that question. Many people have chronic illness. People don't respect their food then they eat it. I guess until we gain a little self-respect, we won't have much respect for those creatures we eat.

There has been increasing awareness about how we raise our food. More and more natural, organic, humanely raised plants and animals are hitting the markets. I still chuckle at the vegetarians that, although they eat vegetables, still are not eating organic. Even though they see how horrific it is to abuse farm raised animals, they don't see that improperly raised plants is a pretty horrific thing also. Conventionally raised plants are grown in nutrient-depleted soils with imbalanced man-made chemical fertilizers and pesticides dumped all over them. What kind of a life is that? When humans have nutrient deficiencies and are overwhelmed with man-made chemical toxins, they get sick, and being sick is not a comfortable thing. Why think that depriving plants of their essential nutrients is a nice thing to do? Some people have this idea that animals are our equals and yet plants are somehow beneath us and it's not ok to kill animals but it's ok to kill plants. Both animals and plants deserve our respect. And each and every one of us deserves some self-respect.

Tests have been done with plants where a polygraph machine was connected to a plant, which is documented in the book *Secret Life of Plants* by Peter Tompkins and Christopher Bird:

> *To see if a plant could display memory, a scheme was devised whereby Backster was to try to identify the secret killer of one of two plants. Six of Backster's polygraph students volunteered for the experiment, some of them veteran policemen. Blindfolded, the students drew from a hat folded slips of paper, on one of which were instructions to root up, stamp on, and thoroughly destroy one of two plants in a room. The criminal was to commit the crime in secret; neither Backster nor any other of the students was to know his identity; only the second plant would be a witness. By attaching the surviving plant to a polygraph and parading the students one by one before it, Backster was able to establish the culprit.*

You can look up Plant perception (paranormal) on Wikipedia for more info on this.

Also, plants can communicate with each other. It's said that if a pest invades a grove of trees, the front line of trees will take the brunt. They may not survive the infestation, but they attempt different ways to protect themselves. When they get it right they communicate the results to the rest of the grove and the rest of the trees make the adjustment and go unscathed.

And we shouldn't even need to hear stories like this to know that plants have feelings and can communicate. Why isn't the fact that we draw lifeforce from them enough to know? And the plants draw lifeforce from the soil. Need I say more down that line? Well, ok, you talked me into it. South Park had a show about the kids getting head lice. They, of course, showed life from the lice's perspective. One louse saw an eyeball looking at him as his host was being inspected. Up until that time, the lice did not realize they existed on a living, breathing, sentient being. This louse attempted to enlighten his buddies to this fact, but they wouldn't believe him that the "world" was alive. Great analogy. Our world, our planet is a living creature also, obviously a being that exhibits one hell of a lot of patience and unconditional love to put up with all our ignorance and abuses.

Like I've said, most of us are still not living off of air or sunlight. Until we raise our frequency to live in some other way, we depend upon taking the life of other beings to sustain our own life. Let's give our food the respect it deserves and, in turn give our own bodies the respect they deserve.

We have so abandoned the fundamentals of diet and lifestyle. I love the literalness of words. Let's look at that word - fundamental. The first part is "fun." That should be our top priority. "If it ain't fun, don't do it." Why take on unnecessary stress and worry ourselves to death? Why consume things that make us feel miserable? Then the next part of fundamental is "duh." The fundamentals last because they work. Nature provides us with everything we need and yet humans think that we can somehow do it all better than nature itself. Talk about conditioning. How'd we all get bamboozled into thinking the food industry could "improve" food. And that brings us to the last part of fundamental – "mental." Keep your head in the game. We start with our health then we remove proper diet and lifestyle then lose our health. We take that proper diet and lifestyle and effectively hide it behind our own back as we look everywhere to see what will give us our health back. Will it be technology with all sorts of gadgetry to diagnose or "fix" the dis-ease that doesn't even need to be there in the first place? The body itself will tell us everything we need to know about its state of health if we'd just learn to listen. People know how to read faces, palms, irises of the eyes, the feet, the bumps on one's head, etc., etc. Will the answer to our ill health be pharmaceuticals or surgery? As Dr. Lorraine Day says, (chuckle) we don't lose our health due to a deficiency of drugs or surgery. How's about we just put back in what we took out in the first place - the fundamentals of proper diet and lifestyle. Doh!

But our lifeforce depends upon more than just food. I saw a heavyset comedian on Last Comic Standing. He said his friends say, "Why are you breathing heavy?" He answers, "To live." This is more literal and more profound than may appear on the surface. I've always been athletic. I've been out hiking up hills with folks who are not very athletic and they are struggling a bit. As I climb, I work with my body, instead of beating against it, and breathe deep to nourish my body with oxygen. I, like this comedian, have had my friends ask me why I'm breathing so heavy. It's not that I am having trouble breathing. It's quite the opposite. And yet they question me because they can hear me breathing. We humans have been so conditioned to not live that we even suppress our breath, even when exerting ourselves. It's bad enough that we live far more sedentary lives than our ancestors and breathe very shallowly when not moving much, but to even do so when exerting ourselves is ludicrous. It's as if it's not socially acceptable to be heard breathing. It's just one more data point of how we're scared to even show any signs of life.

We're having to relearn how to fuel our bodies properly. We've forgotten proper food combining on top of eating poor quality food. We also have forgotten that we absolutely NEED water and sea salt. Talk about fundamental. For every 50 lbs of body weight, we need at least one quart of water per day. So if you weigh 150 lbs, you need 3 quarts of water MINIMUM, more if you are exerting yourself or it's hot out. And that water should not be ice water unless it is very hot out, then our bodies can use our stomach as cooling pumps, but, otherwise consuming very hot or cold things is not ideal. For every quart of water, we need 1/4 teaspoon of sea salt. So many body functions depend on water, sea salt (NOT table salt) and the minerals from the sea salt. Fereydoon Batmanghelidj (www.watercure.com) learned about just how important water and sea salt are to health when he was a political prisoner in Iran years ago and was told to treat fellow prisoners' ailments with limited supplies. Look up Batmanghelidj and the Water Cure to learn how dis-eases like asthma, lupus, allergies, arthritis, etc. can be "cured" just by getting back to the fundamentals that work. Huh. Go figure.

And we are literally being poisoned slowly through our water supply. Yep, "...must be something in the water." It's no exaggeration to say that our health is being adversely affected on all levels - physical, mental, emotional and spiritual. Fluoride represents an example of this quadruple whammy. It is affecting our physical health, but also disrupts our mental capacity and affects us spiritually, which then in turn affects our emotions. As I said in Demonization of Sex, the pituitary is where orgasm happens. Kundalini or sexual energy and orgasm naturally connect us to spirit. Perhaps, needless to say, sex and orgasm are most certainly pleasurable. It's just one of many things that are. Fluoride causes the pituitary gland to calcify. This reduces our pleasurable experiences and, since the pituitary is associated with our 7th and / or 6th chakras, this calcification is depleting our connection to spirit.

Pharmaceuticals are also playing a role in this disconnect. All this disconnection from spirit is causing us emotional trauma also. Walter Cruttenden speaks of an experiment done where people were put in a room that was a Faraday cage. Essentially, it is a metal box that is shielding those inside from electro-magnetic fields and cosmic rays, basically disconnecting the subjects from spirit. In fairly short order, they became very emotionally distressed. A real world example of this are school aged children, most especially boys, that, due to psychological conditioning, restrictions, creativity-inhibiting rules and pharmaceuticals, are getting very depressed because their pituitary glands are adversely affected and this disconnects them from spirit. Yep, for spiritual beings, that can be very depressing.

If you want many gruesome details on fluoride, go to this article and get your fill. *Fluoride –The Battle of Darkness & Light* by Mary Sparrowdancer (www.rense.com/general45/bll.htm). Mary also discusses the importance of proper diet and nutrition and how improper diet, stress and fluoride are all working together to make us quite dysfunctional at all levels by upsetting our biological chemical balance.

And fluoride is, of course, put in conventional toothpastes, but it's not the only health depleting substance in toothpaste. Sodium laurel sulfate, which is a nitrate activator (chemicals working together), is even put in so called "natural" toothpastes. Sodium laurel sulfate is the same cleaner that is used to degrease your car engine. I had to chuckle when I saw that someone made the comment on a website that they finally get this - the food we're being fed is so nasty that they figure we need an engine degreaser to get our teeth clean.

Elaine Smitha, on her TV program Evolving Ideas, interviewed a man who used to do conventional landscaping work. Of course, he was exposed to many different chemicals. His health suffered because of it. He learned about how chemicals work together to cause more harm than they could cause on their own, just one. He learned that the CDC (Center for Disease Control) and the EPA (Environmental Protection Agency) were both well aware of this and yet they don't seem to care to put much effort into enlightening the public to this. This so reminds me of the first Batman movie where Jack Nicholson played the Joker. The Joker wanted to poison the public. He considered poisoning the water supply, but, if only one source were poisoned, then the authorities would catch on in a hurry. So he decided to put a little in the lotion, a little in the soap, a little in the shaving cream, a little in the aftershave, a little in the shampoo. If that isn't art imitating life.

As I've said, our bodies have much to communicate to us. Our tonsils provide our bodies and ourselves with warnings about the food we are eating. If you eat something that causes your tonsils to be swollen or irritated, it's your body's way of saying, "That thing you just ate there, don't eat that." The tonsils then warn the rest of the body, "Get ready, here it comes!" But since humans don't know as much as their own bodies do, instead of not consuming that thing that causes the reaction, they instead rip out the warning light, their tonsils. Most people wouldn't consider doing this in their car. They'd want to find out WHY the warning light was coming on.

When you first start cleaning up your diet and lifestyle, you notice the positive, supportive energy from your food and your healthy way of being. After you've cleaned up your act enough, what sticks out then is not the "good" stuff, but the "bad" stuff. If you take in something else that's good, well, it's just another good thing. But when you do those unhealthy things, you feel it and feel it quickly. It's easy to pinpoint what's not working, be it food, friends, habits, etc. Ah yes, back to trusting our senses again since those uncomfortable things now stick out rather than just being one more of many.

OTHER HEALTH ISSUES

Dogtor J says there are three things involved with cancer – a carcinogen, a virus and a compromised or depleted immune system. This is why some folks can be exposed to a carcinogen and get sick and the next person who's exposed doesn't. Perhaps the one that didn't get sick had a properly functioning immune system due to proper diet and lifestyle and / or they did not contract the virus necessary. The carcinogen acts as a trigger, but is not necessarily the "cause" of the cancer.

Viruses are now being discovered to be involved in many illnesses. Here, again, they are involved, but not necessarily the cause. Different species of animals carry different kinds of viruses based on their own specific body functions, such as body temperature. Dogtor J said that cats' normal body temperature is what we, and the viruses we carry, would consider a "fever," henceforth human viruses cannot live in cats. Now, this is interesting and may give the original reason behind kosher laws not allowing for the consumption of pork. Pigs and humans can readily exchange viruses. So we can get sick from eating a pig with a virus, but we may not get sick from eating another animal with their own virus, which would not survive in the environment of the human body. By not eating pork at all, we just removed one factor that could contribute to our illness – the virus.

A depleted or compromised immune system would be the third factor. You could be exposed to a carcinogen and a virus and yet if you have a properly functioning immune system you won't contract a dis-ease.

This leads into some of the brainwashing surrounding AIDS. People are led to believe that a person gets HIV and that causes their immune system to not function properly. It's quite the opposite.

Through poor diet and lifestyle (including unnecessary stress like living constantly in fight or flight mode when there are no bears chasing them down), a person depletes their immune system. This then allows for what would otherwise be a harmless virus called HIV to then give the person the illness we call AIDS.

Dr. Lorraine Day talks about how little buggies are our friends. Bacteria and viruses only eat dead cells. They do NOT eat living tissue. They're doing us a favor by cleaning dead cells out of our bodies. In the process of munching our dead cells, their digestion releases toxins into our system. Our bodies are built to handle this (if we are eating and living right), no problem. Unfortunately, due to many folks' poor diet and lifestyle, they generate a whole lot of dead cells all at once and this poor diet and lifestyle also contributes to their immune systems not working properly. This means a whole lot of toxins dumped into their systems from the buggies eating so many dead cells. We've no one but ourselves to blame.

Lorraine also talks about studies done with decomposition bacteria. Lab animals have been put into a sealed area that was supposedly free of decomposition bacteria. The animal died and yet the buggies were working on decomposing them immediately. Where did the buggies come from? They were always there. They ARE always there, along with many other viruses and bacteria. People get paranoid about being around someone with a cold and won't shake hands, etc. This is silly. Those buggies are around us and in us ALWAYS. If we eat and live right, which, in turn, allows for our immune system to work properly, then there's no reason for concern. I've experienced folks who won't shake my hand because they have a cold and I tell them, "I can't get your dis-ease. It's yours, not mine." Now, if I have a similar dis-ease, as in lack of ease, their buggies may very well affect me. If I eat as poorly as they do or if I have emotional and mental energies and fears that are similar to theirs (same vibration), then, yes, indeed, I may very well get sick also. But that has nothing to do with them or touching. It's my issue, my responsibility.

This quote from Mark Twain can apply to this topic also, "Soap and education, not as sudden as a massacre, but just as deadly in the long run." Another line that we could add onto this would be, "The cure is worse than the disease." People are using all manner of chemicals to combat buggies, like anti-bacterial soaps, as one example, and these soaps do more harm than good. They kill off the beneficial bacteria that our bodies depend on for so many functions. They mess with our immune systems and make us MORE susceptible to getting "sick" than we would be if we didn't use them. I have a friend who knows a nurse who gets mad about anti-bacterial soaps being peddled to Joe Average. These soaps were never meant for daily use. They were to be used by surgeons just before surgery.

Yep, buggies are our friends. Some hospitals now will use maggots to clean out a gangrenous wound. Like viruses and bacteria, the maggots only eat the dead tissue, not living tissue. Leaving dead, rotting tissue in our bodies will cause much harm. Another example of this that is promoted by dentistry is root canals. By removing the root, the tooth is now dead. It cannot get circulation without its roots. It's just exactly the same as having gangrene and people with root canals often get sick from having this dead tissue sitting in their bodies.

And buggies work the same way in animals also. If you feed your animals properly, which unfortunately does not involve "pet food", they are not as susceptible to getting fleas or mites or worms. And yet those creatures are doing the same thing the little buggies are. Those parasites are the "scavengers" of the body and are there having a hay day because there are an overabundance of dead cells to munch and a depleted immune system that's not strong enough to deal.

Pet food is as bad or worse than conventional human food. Some of the low-end pet foods even use rendered animals. That sometimes means animals that died from disease. Most carnivores would not eat something like that if they found it out in nature unless there was absolutely nothing else to eat. They probably still would turn their noses up at it in pet food if those pet foods weren't loaded with artificial flavorings to trick them into eating it. Sometimes the rendered animals used even include the same species of animal that it is meant to be fed to. So now they are turning our pets into cannibals. Since learning that they may even be putting diseased cat and dog meat in cat and dog food, if I have had to have a vet put a pet down, I do not opt for them to be turned over to rendering plants, I have them cremated. This kind of practice is what mad cow disease springs from. They're feeding diseased cow meat to cows. And cows aren't even carnivores. This is beyond sick. What's next, Soylent Green? Christ, at this point, are we sure we're not eating Soylent Green? That's a scary thought, but, if I weren't here on this planet actually witnessing what does go on I wouldn't believe some of this absurdity either.

Pet food, just like packaged human food, is also loaded with what Dogtor J calls the Four Horsemen of the Apocalypse - soy, gluten, dairy, and corn - which are the four biggest "food" (use that term loosely) allergens. Neither man nor beast has any business eating these things or considering them food. I feed my carnivore cat all natural meat and fish. He's very healthy. His coat is smooth and shiny. His coat and paw pads don't get dried out. He is svelte and fit. He has his moments, but, for the most part, he often shows no sign of parasites. He lives in the same yard as my neighbor's cat. The neighbor feeds her cat pet food. He is obese and his coat is dry and rough with patches missing. He obviously has fleas and skin problems as he struggles to maneuver his obese body around to scratch. They are in the same environment and yet one is overrun with parasites and the other isn't.

And yet parasites, just like viruses and bacteria, have their place in our health. Recently an article put out by Jane E. Brody called *"Eating dirt can be good for you – just ask babies"* presents information from studies on this topic.

> *"What a child is doing when he puts things in his mouth is allowing his immune response to explore his environment," Mary Ruebush, a microbiology and immunology instructor, wrote in her new book, "Why Dirt Is Good" (Kaplan). "Not only does this allow for 'practice' of immune responses, which will be necessary for protection, but it also plays a critical role in teaching the immature immune response what is best ignored."*

> *One leading researcher, Dr. Joel Weinstock, the director of gastroenterology and hepatology at Tufts Medical Center in Boston, said in an interview that the immune system at birth "is like an unprogrammed computer. It need instruction."*

> *He said that public health measures like cleaning up contaminated water and food have saved the lives of*

countless children, but they "also eliminated exposure to many organisms that are probably good for us."

"Children raised in an ultra-clean environment," he added, "are not being exposed to organisms that help them develop appropriate immune regulatory circuits."

What comes to mind here for me is the word "balance." There's a difference between hygiene and paranoia.

Studies he has conducted with Dr. David Elliott, a gastroenterologist and immunologist at the University of Iowa, indicate that intestinal worms, which have been all but eliminated in developed countries, are "likely to be the biggest player" in regulating the immune system to respond appropriately, Elliott said in an interview. He added that bacterial and viral infections seem to influence the immune system in the same way, but not as forcefully.

Most worms are harmless, especially in well-nourished people, Weinstock said. "There are very few diseases that people get from worms," he said. "Humans have adapted to the presence of most of them."

Ya didn't have to tell this farm girl that. I've eaten so much dirt and so many insects also and know that other people have too, whether they realize it or not. As a kid, I used to think that the grain hopper on a combine (combination cutter / thrasher) used to gather grain was called a "hopper" because it had so many grasshoppers in it. I've never kidded myself that breads and such aren't loaded with bug parts. Mmmm mm. Extra protein.

Like I talked about under the heading of Demonization of Money, the money involved in the food, pharmaceutical and health industries, the oil and chemical industries, the cell phone industry, etc., is not the end, it's not the beginning either, it's only part of the means. The real reason for these entities to do what they do, to make us think we can't live without drugs, surgery, chemicals and other harmful things, is not about money. They WANT to make our planet and us unhealthy. Now, of course, I'm talking about the people at the top who know what they're doing. Joe Average working in these industries often has no clue and / or just needs to pay the bills, but they aren't the ones rolling in dough, so it's rather tough to say "it's all about money" about them anyway. The ill health created by these industries is not a side effect of being money hungry. It's not happenstance. It's not fallout. It's the original reason for these goings on. Keeping us unhealthy keeps us from realizing our full potential of being the Christs, the gods, the soul resurrection machines we were designed to be.

As people like Dr. Lorraine Day have found out, the "cure" is to get it right in the first place and, even if you get it all wrong and are on your deathbed, getting it right can turn your health around. But even though fundamentals of diet and lifestyle are the ultimate answer, there have been many methods found to cure dis-ease like cancer and give you a fresh start, set all the meters back to zero, if you will. And yet those cures have been "covered up" or people and businesses destroyed by those that would try to control us.

One such method is talked about by Tom Bearden (www.cheniere.org). Tom is ex-military. He knows that scalar / longitudinal waves can be used to make cancer cells literally go back in time to before they were cancer cells - cancer cure! Yeah, I know, it sounds like science fiction, but science fiction is often based on reality that the mass of people just aren't aware of yet. In the last century, we've seen decades old sci-fi become part of our everyday lives.

Tie this into standing serpent waves that William Henry speaks of in his mythology research. Truth is, though, that these scalar / serpent waves may not need to be delivered to us through some medical machinery, but are available to us always. We just need to learn / re-member how to do so, and we are, each and every one of us, well equipped to do so.

Also some folks have spoken of how MRI machines, which are used as a diagnostic tool, can also be used to heal, and they're not being utilized for that.

Italian Oncologist Dr. Tullio Simoncini has discovered that cancer is a fungus. Well, this certainly resonates with me, as I know that yeast infections are very common for folks indulging in the SAD (standard American diet). All the refined and processed foods which are high carb are creating an environment that the yeast can thrive in. Like previously mentioned, yeasts are always in our bodies, but beneficial bacteria in our system help to keep the yeast populations from exploding. When we do things that deplete our beneficial bacteria (like antibiotics) and support the yeast, our bodies get out of balance. The tumors our bodies produce are the body's way of enclosing a yeast infection gone wild. It's about protecting itself from all that yeast.

Well, Tullio Simoncini realized that anti-fungal medicine only goes so far to help rid the body of yeast because the fungus can mutate to adapt and does so fairly quickly. He knows that yeast thrive in an acid environment. This correlates with other information that knows that cancer is associated with a high acid pH in the body. Tullio uses a catheter to go down a main artery to douse the tumors in simple baking soda that creates a highly alkaline environment that the fungus cannot survive in. Now, a person really should not count on getting tumors doused in baking soda repeatedly to survive on an on-going basis, but, if it's a life or death situation, this treatment can provide for a fresh start. The person then needs to change their diet and lifestyle so as not to re-create the conditions that allow yeast to thrive. And what has this approach won for Tullio? He has had his medical license yanked. This is how the conventional modern medicine world is. They don't want people to be healthy. That doesn't serve their purposes. They will do anything they deem necessary to keep real cures from getting to the general populace. Tullio's lawyers are working to get him reinstated. See video by searching on "Mercola fungus causing cancer."

Another thing causing ill health is vaccinations. Most, if not all, vaccines, still contain mercury and other harmful substances. And even without that, the whole concept of vaccinations beats against the body's natural defense systems. The body revs up its immune response as it takes in the infectious agent through natural means, like through the sinuses and lungs, or through the skin. Vaccines inject the infection directly into cells, bypassing the body's natural defenses.

A while back, there was a big hubbub about people concerned about others who do not want their children to have the measles shot and whether those unpoked children should then be allowed in public schools. Oh please. I tell folks they need to make up their minds about whether the measles shot works or not. If it does work and they give the shot to their own children, then what does it matter that children without the shot go to the same school. Isn't that why they give the shot, to protect the recipient from measles if exposed to it? If the shot works, then the recipient should be able to live in a world full of measles and not get it... right? Does it work or doesn't it? These folks could stand to listen to themselves, to how their reasoning contradicts itself.

Ex military nurse Joyce Riley (www.gulfwarvets.com) works to expose the real causes of Gulf War Syndrome. There are many factors involved. At the top of the list is the anthrax vaccine. First of all, vaccines are not good in a general sense as they bypass the body's normal defense mechanisms. Joyce came across the work of a doctor who had figured out why breast implants were making women sick. She realized that the adjuvant in the anthrax vaccine was the same petroleum base that was used in breast implants. That was really doing a number on people's immune systems.

The Gulf War vets were also exposed to depleted uranium. The soldiers were so uneducated about the dangers of depleted uranium that they would take Iraqi tank pieces that had been shelled with depleted uranium weapons home to their kids as souvenirs. These contaminated parts may even have been stored under their children's beds. These soldiers, basically, unknowingly, took Gulf War Syndrome home to their families who are also getting sick.

The soldiers were also exposed to biological and chemical warfare from both enemy and friendly fire and, in some cases soldiers were ordered NOT to don their protective gear when a friendly fire weapon was being launched. Some commanders refused to give that order to their soldiers. Those soldiers did not suffer the consequences that those exposed did. Those commanders have faced court martial for doing the right thing.

One more item that contributed was that pallets of diet pop containing aspartame were dropped out in the desert heat for the soldiers to consume. Aspartame is just flat toxic and most especially in liquid form, like in pop, it easily converts to methanol / formaldehyde when above temperatures in the 80s Fahrenheit. So there those pallets sat, out in the desert hear. Well, even the human body is 98.6 degrees Fahrenheit, so just consume it and you've set up the environment for that conversion.

To add even more horrors to this whole situation, those soldiers who are sick or traumatized are being put on antidepressants. In many cases their physical level illness is not even being treated. They're just being told they have posttraumatic stress disorder (PTSD) and the antidepressants are all they get. Antidepressants can be very dangerous, most especially when people have developed a dependency on them and then suddenly go off of them. Many times, this results in murder / suicide. Ex-military personnel are literally killing their families and then themselves. Some don't quite get to the suicide part when they "wake up" and realize everyone in the house is dead and they have no memory of what happened. This has gotten to be so commonplace that when police officers and detectives arrive on the scene, they look around at their fellow officers and ask, "Anyone find the Prozac yet?"

If you or someone you know has ill health since serving in the gulf, look up Joyce Riley and she'll direct you to some real help.

Bruce Lipton said the number of deaths due to prescription drugs every year is 300,000 people. And, the leading cause of death, far outweighing heart disease, is medical intervention. Bruce said 740,000 people per year are killed by medical intervention. Watch the interview with Bruce Lipton on CMN - Conscious Media Network.

Dr. Leonard Horowitz has observed that the threat of so-called pandemics comes with a major propaganda campaign by the mainstream / establishment. They're using fear mongering to make people sick. Some examples of this are the propaganda campaigns that came with influenza during WWI, the avian flu and, of course, the yearly announcement of "cold and flu season." So, this is playing on the fact that many people have been conditioned to be very germ paranoid. The germs won't get ya, but the paranoia will. And that makes for a nice segue into the next topic.

OUR BELIEFS AS OUR ENVIRONMENT

As cellular biologist Bruce Lipton discusses in his book *Biology of Belief*, our DNA does not rule our bodies and health, for the most part, as both scientists and laymen alike have been led to believe. It is our environment that determines our health. Our cells, and the larger cell of our entire being, respond to their environment. The DNA provides the "blueprint" to instruct cell proteins on how to handle changes in environment, but the DNA is not "controlling" anything. Bruce said you couldn't take a blueprint and throw it out on the ground and expect a building to pop up. The blueprint just tells the construction workers how to build the building, but it's the workers that make it happen. It's the cell membrane that senses the environment and the cell proteins read the blueprint of DNA and determine the cell's (and, henceforth our bodies') functions and responses.

Our thoughts, feelings and beliefs are a very large part of our cells' environment. Henry Ford said one person might believe something can be and another person doesn't - both are right. We are creating our own realities. We put energy behind our beliefs and, gee, watch what manifests. Everything starts at the energetic level. Apply enough mental and emotional energy at a high enough level and / or over a long enough period of time and it will most certainly manifest at the physical level. As I talked about earlier in Demonization of Our Bodies, Louise Hay, in her book, *Heal Your Body*, helps us to interpret what our bodies are telling us about the mental energy behind our physical afflictions. Take heed to what your body is communicating to you.

Bruce says there are basically 3 perceptions of our environment - growth opportunity, threat (protection mode) or neutral (background music). The body's cells (and our entire being) move towards growth opportunities and away from threats. But what's important is the word "perception". What came into my mind is Michael Tsarion's line about that disempowered conditional state of "teacher = threat." If we perceive as a threat those people and circumstances that, in reality, are growth opportunities, we just missed the opportunity. Dual meaning of Chaos - Crisis and Opportunity. Which do we choose to view it as?

And Bruce gives the scientific observation of what spiritualists have known since the word go - love is the stimulus for growth / opening up, and fear is the stimulus for protection / closing off. Love will make us want to move towards it, through Hell and high water, scaling mountains to get to it. "River deep, mountain high", as Tina Turner sang.

Bruce observed that a cell cannot be in both growth mode and protection mode at the same time, cannot be both open and closed at the same time, cannot be both moving towards and moving away from outside stimulus. The entire organism, the human body, behaves in the same manner as the individual cells - as above, so below - the holographic nature of everything. We, as human beings, also cannot be in growth mode and protection mode at the same time. When we are in constant fight or flight mode due to the "perceived" threat of our environment when, in reality, there is no threat, we are actually slowly killing ourselves because we are not growing, not creating, not getting blood to all parts of our bodies and also not replacing cells, etc. If there really was a bear chasing you, the common cold you have is not as high priority as the bear, so the immune system also shuts down. But if the "threat" is only perceived and not real, and this perception is constant we're dying, not living.

Another lower priority body function, when in fight or flight mode, is the reproduction system. It's really not all that critical to be making babies when that bear is chasing you down. I knew someone that was having almost constant menstruation. She was stressed, worked a lot, overdid substances that were not healthy and it was all about dodging her issues. Her diet and lifestyle were escapes from her wounds and issues. Her body was screaming at her to make a change. Her solution? Rip out the "offending" body part. She had a hysterectomy. She did not stop working so much, did not reduce stress in her life, did not quit abusing her body with harmful substances, and did not tend to her healing. Nothing changed for her except that now she doesn't have a uterus. Dr. Lorraine Day says this type of thing would be like taking your car to a mechanic because the transmission is not working and the mechanic takes your transmission out and gives you your car back. We don't have spare body parts. When the warning light in your car comes on, you set about to find out why. You don't rip out the warning light. Doesn't your body and your entire being deserve at least as much respect and care as your car?

Bruce speaks of the HPA axis, which stands for hypothalamus / pituitary / adrenals. The hypothalamus interprets the perception. The pituitary or "master gland" gets the info to all cells. If in protection / threat mode, the adrenals send out stress hormones. Arms and legs are nourished in a "fight or flight" mode. But the energy is shifted away from other body parts, away from growth, maintenance and immune functions. Like I wrote about in the Other Health Issues section, Bruce says that every organism that can affect human health is ALWAYS there. Any blood test would verify this. It's not something we "catch" from someone or something else. They are called "opportunistic" organisms, as they are always there just waiting for the immune system to not be functioning properly so they can multiply and thrive. So a constant fight or flight way of being or staying in a stressful environment unnecessarily is allowing for these buggies to cause illness. Look out for yourself. If you're dreaming up stress that isn't there, do what it takes to correct your stinkin' thinkin'. If you are in a truly stressful environment, perhaps it's time to remove yourself from it before it literally kills you.

Neil Slade, in his book The Frontal Lobes Supercharge, talks about the amygdalae in our brains, which serve as switches. This is that same kind of situation that Bruce Lipton speaks of with the HTP axis. The amygdalae (Greek for almond, as they are almond-shaped) sit behind our eyes, about an inch inside our temples. They are switches that switch between the reptilian brain and the frontal lobes. The reptilian brain is concerned about survival. It's that "fight or flight" part of our brain. The frontal lobes are about creativity and growth. Here, again, the reptilian mind certainly has its place. If a bear really is chasing you down, the reptilian brain kicks in and you can operate at top performance to run away or do whatever is necessary to survive. But we've gotten to the point where we are experiencing so much fear about all myriad of things, even those things that don't even happen, worrying about what might be, that we find ourselves in constant fight or flight mode, constantly "clicked" into reptilian brain. When we are using our reptilian brain, our frontal lobes, and, hence, our growth and creativity, are out of the picture.

If we learn to "click" our amgydalae forward and tap into our frontal lobes, it will help not only our growth and creativity, but also even our survival, as we will anticipate, with a clear mind, any impending dangers long before they become an emergency. Often, this switch is made unconsciously, but we can also do this consciously. A technique that Neil offered was to visualize the amygdalae just behind your eyes (I find that mine are right at the bottom of my eyeball) and an inch inside the temple. Think of a feather tickling that front edge of those almond-shaped switches. That puts you into your frontal lobes and into growth and creation mode. I find that when I get it just right, a spontaneous smile overcomes me.

The frontal lobes are also where our free will comes from. Dr. Joseph Dispenza in *What the Bleep!? Down the Rabbit Hole*, in discussing this, said they've tested people with a choice between two things. They said either was fine, whatever they wanted. They flat could not choose. If they were told one was right and one was wrong, then they could choose. Bottom line - they were choosing based on conditioning, not on free will. They were choosing according to old neural connections of the familiar, rather than kicking in their frontal lobes.

Bruce Lipton states that the brainwave frequency of children, age 6 and under, is a hypnagogic state. It's just like being hypnotized - anything said to them goes right into the subconscious, programmed straight in, which makes sense considering that a young person is learning about the new realm they have entered here on Earth. Unfortunately, if the child's parents and others that they depend on to learn from are not aware of the child being so easily "programmable" and say or do the wrong thing, they may have created wounds in the child that last many years, sometimes an entire lifetime (or beyond).

I have heard it said that at the moment of orgasm, we are in a similar hypnagogic brainwave state. Whatever is said goes right in and stays there. Be kind to your lovers and be mindful of what you say to them at the moment of climax, for it will be planted directly into the subconscious.

The subconscious is very large and fast. It takes care of all the background stuff that we can do almost mindlessly. Most of our adult lives, the brainwave frequency we are usually at requires that we learn things through the conscious mind. The conscious mind is used to program or re-program the subconscious. But the conscious mind is a million times slower and smaller than the subconscious. So, this is why those ideas implanted into us at a young age can be so difficult to change as an adult.

To better understand how the conscious and subconscious work, Bruce offered the example of driving. When we are first learning, we are using our small, slow conscious mind to do so. We have a steering wheel, peddles, gear shift, mirrors, traffic, road signs and lights, and someone sitting next to us barking commands at us all at once and it's a whole lot for our conscious minds to handle. The person in the seat next to us drives with their subconscious since they have driven for years and it's become quite second nature to them and they just can't understand why we can't get this simple task of learning to drive. When this task becomes rote and a function of the subconscious, which is very good at what it does, we can get from home to some destination, sometimes without our conscious mind paying any attention. We may be conversing or just thinking or daydreaming and the next thing we know we're safely at our destination and have no memory of all the sights we passed on the way.

The conventional psychotherapy techniques that are used to identify our original wounds are not enough to actually heal those wounds. Merely knowing when an idea got planted into the subconscious will not reprogram the subconscious. We can use our conscious mind to re-program our subconscious, but that requires a persistent, diligent effort, indeed. We're talking about a lifestyle change that very much starts at the energetic level of thought and emotion. Bruce Lipton states that there are some fast track methods that can help reprogram the subconscious and remove emotional blockages and it's not even necessary that we know what put the original program there. Hypnotherapy, Emotional Freedom Technique (EFT), and Psych-K can be very useful. EFT is something you can do yourself. It's easy to learn and to apply. As I wrote about in the Demonization of Hell section, to see a video interview about EFT with Phillip Mountrose, go to CMN - Conscious Media Network. (www.consciousmedianetwork.com). Gary Craig (www.emofree.com) offers a free EFT manual.

As I said in the section The Human Mind Does Not Register Negation, we often create what we don't want by using negation. This quote from an interview with Gregg Braden speaks of how we create what we don't want by focusing on it:

> *Yes, if we define intention as the act of observing our world with an expectation of an outcome. We are always creating, even when we are not aware of what we are creating. We can't not create! Everywhere we look, consciousness will put something there for us to see. If you are awake and conscious, you are creating. So, what*

*does it mean when you are trained to look for something
you don't want? What does it mean to keep looking for a
lump in a breast?*

Worry is a prayer for what we don't want. Energy flows where
attention goes. Are you truly creating what you want? Bruce
speaks of how we get conditioned to associate certain things to
achieve a desired outcome and yet this can be detrimental. If a
child has parents who take no time for him except when he's sick,
then the child learns to equate getting sick with getting love and
affection. This subconscious association sticks with him as an
adult. He doesn't know on a conscious level why he keeps getting
sick.

As anyone who does Tarot readings has learned from The
Tower card, sometimes what is essential for our continued growth,
healing and our very survival is for our beliefs to be completely
shattered.

*"Listen... it may feel like hell, but sometimes lost is where
you need to be. Just because you don't know your
direction doesn't mean you don't have one."*

From TV Series Battlestar Galactica

The highly conditioned human ego often closely associates self
with beliefs. This is not a healthy association. The conditioned ego
will cling to old, outdated beliefs as a matter of survival. It's not that
we ARE our beliefs, we HAVE beliefs. And if our beliefs get
shattered, we, ourselves, are still just fine. We will not be shattered
with our beliefs. We need not hold on for dear life to beliefs that no
longer serve us.

And, at this point, I'd like to say that we must be careful in our
shift of paradigm to not now demonize the ego. Don't shun your
ego. Too many spiritual folk are doing just that. It's exactly this kind
of thing that made us shun our higher selves and our intuition and
part of why the ego has been so overused and misused and our
intuition and connection to the Divine so underutilized. The ego, like
the rest of our being, has a place, a purpose. It is the ego that
stepped up so many years ago to get the human race past species
and solar system catastrophes and traumas. Without the ego, we
would not have been able to function. We could have easily

become quivering masses of gelatinous human flesh as we buckled under extreme pressures. We wouldn't be here to tell our story without the ego. We can't expect to be whole if we keep demonizing parts of ourselves.

Astrologically speaking, ego-drive has to do with the planet Mars and the sign of Aries. Should we throw out one planet and one sign? Each planet and each sign has its lower and higher energies. A couple of my favorite astrology books talk about the unevolved vs. the evolved versions of each sign. Hallelujah. It has to do with how those energies are applied. Without Mars and the energies of Aries, we would not have drive, action, perseverance, power, will, the fire in our guts. We wouldn't defend ourselves. Without ego, we would not have those things either. Where we really get in trouble is when we allow others to shape and mold our egos. The dysfunctional, disempowering conditioning that humans have been slathered in for far too long is the culprit, not the ego itself. And you can bet that "they" who have dared to try to control us all these millennia would so love to have us do away with our egos. We'd just lie down and take their ab-uses then. That would be the final nail in the coffin of our personal power. If the ego can be conditioned in a dysfunctional, disempowering way, then that same sense of self, which is what the ego is, can also be conditioned in a more empowered way, in a direction that brings in our higher self.

Instead of demonizing the ego, we can lovingly, compassionately ask our egos to chill a bit and that it's time to let our higher selves help out more. Tell the ego to take a much-deserved break and to let loose its grip on the steering wheel sometimes. "Man, am I exhausted. I didn't realize how hard I'd been working until I stopped and let the adrenaline levels fall." Reassure it that by taking a higher perspective on things, your entire being's continued survival will be ensured. And survival is all that the ego has ever really cared about. It's just gotten used to being in charge of that. It's had the rather ungrateful job of juggling between id and super ego, between our passions and our inhibitions in a world where the straight and narrow keeps getting straighter and narrower. We've judged and demonized the light and the dark both. What's left in that reality? Tough balancing act, indeed.

But now there's a different way. We are being offered a chance at attaining a more balanced state, an integrated state, a world where light and dark are not polarities, but complements, which means completion and wholeness. I find that as I lovingly ask my ego along on a different kind of ride and as I more fully reconnect with my higher self, my ego is right there saying such things as, "Sorry, I was tricked." Yes dear ego, the disempowering conditioning has been slathered on thick. Yes, indeed. "What can I do different?" Let the higher self in to help more. "I now want to do more than just survive, I want to thrive." I'm with ya dear ego. "This is fun as all get out." My ego is just as jazzed about this new way of being as the rest of me, as well it should be. Woo hoo.

When I hear from God, my higher self, other parts of my being, Mommy Earth, angels etc., I feel these entities on or near different parts of my body. When I first started talking to my ego, I could not pinpoint its location. As its energy shifts to allow for a more fully integrated self, I can now feel it just to the left of my heart. My sense of self has moved to my heart chakra. Ready for integration! Integrate ego and higher self and look out world, we just reconnected to our power. Mark, get set, go!

> "The 4th chakra is the heart, the center for love, compassion, spirituality."
> "It connects the body, mind and spirit. It integrates the male and the female, the ego and unity."
> "You must work on this chakra a lot."
> "Oh, it's been said I have a huge ego. But it's the ego of the individual that makes change in this world. Greatness lives in those who..."
> "...act."

Dialogue from TV series Saving Grace.

Learn from the parts of your life that ARE working. See how your thoughts and feelings in those areas are different than those areas that aren't working. See how your self-talk differs between these areas. Observe the abundance vs. lack energy. Apply those thoughts and feelings from the areas that work to the areas that don't.

I find that, on any level, a good test for a belief, doesn't matter what the topic is, is this - Is this belief empowering or disempowering? Is this belief self-affirming or self-sabotaging? You and God did not co-create you and put you on this green Earth for you to not be yourself, your TRUE self - not the wounded, dysfunctional, overly egotistical, negatively conditioned and disempowered self, but your TRUE self, the one that is a god or goddess and knows this and accepts their own power and greatness. That true self is the greatest thing you have to offer this world. And this world is in dire need of healing. Help it by helping yourself be yourself.

WALKING ZOMBIES

> *All you zombies show your faces*
> *(I know you're out there)*
> *All you people in the street*
> *(Let's see you)*
> *All you sittin' in high places*
> *It's all gonna fall on you*
>
> *Lyrics from "All You Zombies" by The Hooters*

The Essenes and Gnostics spoke of the unenlightened as "the dead". In the Bible, when there was talk of raising someone from the dead, it may not have been literal. It was not like H.P. Lovecraft's *Re-animator* or Mary Shelley's *Frankenstein*. This terminology was symbolic. "The dead" were given new life as they were awakened to a world that was always around them that they'd just never been consciously aware of before.

We must first awaken to the control agenda that is keeping us down. Then what is more significant is the reasons why that agenda exists. Ultimately, it all comes back to the fact that if we were left to our natural way of being, we would be gods, Christs. And, yet again, as William Henry says, "Christs don't pay their taxes." Yep, Christs are not a very controllable lot. And "they" are very fearful, so they don't like the idea of us not being controllable.

I have to say something at this point though. On the way to becoming a Christ, it's said that Jesus actually did pay his taxes. In the world, and yet not of it. The message being that one can follow the rules of mankind, no matter how absurd those rules are, and still continue with the inner work, with the process of ascension. If nothing else, those outer absurdities can often be the catalyst, the impetus to drive one inward to do the work that really matters. Everything we need is always provided to us. We have every opportunity. We don't need to be part of "their" in crowd to be able to ascend. Everyone in every class, in every race and culture, has the opportunity to pull this off. The question is, will we actually capitalize on the opportunities that Life and the Divine provide to us?

When I write about Walking Zombies, I always capitalize that title. I have great respect for Walking Zombies. I've had that experience myself. Like so many others, I ultimately came here to be triggered into awakening and to play a role in passing that potential awakening on to the next human.

Nicole Whitney of News for the Soul interviewed Dr. Lee Pulos (drpulos.com). He spoke of much the same kind of thing that I'm discussing in this book, as far as beliefs creating our own reality and the effects on the quantum and physical levels. Just as Bruce Lipton speaks of, Lee stated that at a young age we are literally hypnotized. So if that cultural hypnotism makes us think that we are not capable of great things, then we don't do those great things. But we can de-hypnotize ourselves and do things like teleportation, change the molecular structure of substances and many other things that many think are not achievable. At one point, he talked about how the Buddha was asked if he was a god or an angel. Buddha answered that he was neither, he was just awake. Lee said you break out of old beliefs by exposing yourself to new information, by looking at the world with fresh eyes.

I'd like to elucidate a slightly different angle to the point made by Buddha though, since applying the labels of god or angel to someone often has a lot of old conditioned societal baggage clinging to it, the conditioning being that to be a god or an angel is unique, like it's not something that applies to everyone. We've been conditioned to think that someone claiming to be a god or an angel is saying they are better than the rest of us. I beg to differ and I'm sure the Buddha did not want to imply that he was unique or superhuman either. He was human and was demonstrating what humans can do. He was awake though, which not everyone is awake, but they can be, the potential is there. I think we all are gods and angels. It's just that not everyone is awake to that fact. Therein lies the significant difference. Just wake up to how great we are and suddenly we're doing great things, things that Christs and Buddhas do, a potential that is always within all of us, not just reserved for a few.

THE GLOBAL CONTROL AGENDA

A fun website for the working class dog and their managers and executives is despair.com, which uses satire to show their disgust for motivational posters that many corporations like to put on display. One of their cards is titled Propaganda and says, "What Lies Behind Us and Before Us are Small Matters Compared to What Lies Right to Our Faces."

And the best place to hide something is in plain view.

I thought of the following analogy of the world's events: I could ask this line of questioning to people - if you had a small child who was being molested would you not want that to stop? And what if you were not aware it was going on, how could you stop something you don't even know is going on? And at the next level, if you knew it was happening, but didn't know who was doing it, would you now be suspicious of everyone and be rather mean to everyone since they could be the molesters? This is how this world has been controlled - divide and conquer. Some folks don't know of some of the abuses in the world. Then if they know the abuse exists, they don't know who is ultimately responsible, although they think they do, and so want to lash out at everyone around them. Now they are passing on the abuse. All that infighting is what allows the few to control the many.

Now, with the global issues, it will take more than just one person to awaken to the abuses and who is responsible. It will take a critical mass of people to awaken before change will occur in a profound way. This is why we learn as much as we can and we also share as much of that information as we can. It has to start at the awareness level. You can't go reeling out of control like a loose cannon and lash out at everyone. That just causes more problems. You then become the abuser yourself. You also cannot go willy-nilly putting band-aids on every problem in the world and never address the ultimate source of the problems or you'll just be chasing your tail, wearing yourself out, without making a significant change for the better. If you knock yourself out, you're no longer of any use to this world. And, like I said in the Preface, most things that people think are problems are not really problems in and of themselves, but *symptoms* of the real problems.

The movie Mindwalk, which was filmed in 1991 and is still cutting edge, brings up the topic of how we can't just look at each "problem" as its own thing. Everything is interconnected. We have to change our perception, perspectives and attitudes at a fundamental level in order to truly turn this world around. It will take these fundamental changes in order to address EVERYTHING that must be addressed. Starting anywhere other than our perception will only be a superficial band-aid and some of us (not all) are quickly approaching the point of no return. The positive changes we make now will result in our personal and species evolution instead of create our own extinction by continuing down the road we've been on. I highly recommend the movie Mindwalk. It will make you think, just as the characters made each other think.

There has been a hidden hand at work in this world for a very long time, since even before what we have come to know as modern man (after the "missing link") has been around. Some would say "conspiracy" and there are definitely lots of those, but they are merely subsets of a larger global agenda. And as Credo Mutwa told David Icke (www.davidicke.com) in Reptilian Agenda, we could stand to quit calling such things "theories." Theories don't kill people and influence world events, but conspiracies do. All facets of our lives have been influenced by this control agenda - be it through religion, science, education, government (which literally means "control mind"), politics, media, commerce, big business, banking, food, water, modern medicine, alteration of history, etc. The same hidden hand is at work at the top of all these organizations and this influences decisions made about our collective society. There is no left vs. right or this country vs. that country. The Seattle Weekly nailed it with an article put out around the time of the WTO (World Trade Organization) conference and protest in 1999 - it's "top vs. bottom." It's the rulers / establishment / global elite vs. the rest of us.

I say that these people at the top influence us because no one can truly take authority over us, but we most certainly can give it away. And we have done so in a very big way. It's taken a long time to get to this level of conditioning and dysfunction, but here we are collectively and the symptoms can be seen everywhere.

People are animals and just like animals can sense fear. Even if they are not consciously aware of their own sensing of your fear, they still do and may "attack" you in a variety of ways until you show them your spine, as if a part of them very much wants you to show them your power. I can't help but think that our leaders are like this to some degree, again, even if they are not consciously aware of it. They blatantly flaunt their ab-use right before our eyes, almost disbelieving that they can get away with it for so long and so fully. They probably think most people are a bunch of saps and yet, perhaps, there is a part of them that unconsciously, at this point in time, is just seeing how far they have to push us to wake us up.

"But what about the children" gets used to tweak on people's emotions and gets them to do things that really are NOT in the children's (or anyone's) best interest. The methods used, truth be known, are doing more harm than good, like the education system as one example. If folks knew how disempowering the education system is, they'd want to dismantle it in a hurry. And disempowerment, a dumbing down, was exactly the original intent of those who started the public education system. The "but what about the children" scheme is just one small example of how fear is used to herd people where "they" want them.

And the establishment knows that big wheels turn slow. They can put some harmful thing into the works and even if someone discovers it fairly soon, it will take a while before those that want to change things can build up steam and get enough other people on board to make it happen. There was lead in gasoline for many years before enough people became aware and put enough pressure on to get that changed. Meanwhile, all through those years, the damage is being done. The same applies to such things as tobacco, "food", pharmaceuticals, and cell phones. Several people have to get sick and / or die before any change is made.

I do so love though to see the enlightened folks strutting their personal power when they see the opportunity. A while back when states were suing the tobacco industry for health care costs, I saw a man from MIT being interviewed on TV about the tobacco industry. He was so demonizing it, which it well should be, but it was as if to say that all of our health issues are due to tobacco in some way, even for those that don't smoke. I had to chuckle at this guy just a squirming in his chair as a caller told him, yes, indeed, tobacco was nasty, but what about how the food industry is poisoning everyone. He raked this so-called expert up one side and down the other. It was a pleasure to behold. What can I say? Watching someone step out of fear, speak their truth, speak up for themselves and their fellow human, even against the odds, just gives me such joy. This is what these significant times are about - people awakening and rediscovering their own personal power. Courage and Joy are soul-centered qualities and it's wonderful to see people have the Courage to bring Joy to the world, to bring Heaven to Earth, which is the end result of speaking their truth.

Like I said before, the establishment's "job" of keeping us disempowered is an endless job. They HAVE to keep after it. If left to be, without this constant barrage of psychic, emotional and physical poisoning, we'd eventually, naturally roll back into being the Christs that we are, and all of the absurdities of Life here on Earth would eventually come to an end.

Most people think that the Roman Empire is long gone. Not so. It morphed into the Catholic Church - ya know, the *Roman* Catholic Church. John Paul I, bless his soul, wanted to roll heads and clean up the corruption in the Vatican and throughout the church worldwide, so his cardinals promptly killed him. John Paul II saw that cleaning house was then not the way to go if he actually wanted to remain in this world to help it and I swear that man lived as long as he did, in such poor health, just so he could do his best to slow down "their" agenda, to stall as best he could the control the establishment exerts through the Vatican.

Aaron Russo, with his film Freedom to Fascism, showed just how free we are - not! Or how not free we will be if we continue down the path we're on. Russo pointed out, as David Icke and Michael Tsarion and many others that the world banking system lends (no pun intended) to a very large part of the establishment's control agenda. It's so good to see that someone like Aaron has made a major motion picture to disclose this world control.

Since I just mentioned these two factions of the global elite / establishment, I'll say this – I recently read an article about who

109

backed both sides of the American civil war. World bankers backed the north. The Vatican backed the south. These fargin power hungry bastages squabble amongst themselves and wage war on each other and the mass of people are their expendable pawns.

Michael Moore's movie Sicko demonstrates just how truly brainwashed, propagandized and information-isolated people are in the United States. The media control over information about other countries has led many Americans to think that we're at the top of the heap and other countries are so behind and backward. Again... not! Our media, government, and health care system have folks thinking we have the greatest health care system in the world. People who have moved to France, England and even Cuba know better. Check out Moore's site for information on how far down the list the U.S. health care system and our health really are, even behind countries that Americans consider "third world." I personally wonder about Michael Moore and his motives, conditioning, fear levels and level of awareness (or lack thereof), but I have got to highly recommend Sicko. Perhaps Michael too is starting to see just how far-reaching this global control agenda is.

There are those folks who are aware of the establishment's global agenda with all its deceit who want the establishment to disclose the truth and to be punished for their lies. These times are not about punishing those that have "done unto" us. It's not about revenge. It's not about them fessing up to anything, although they have done that over time, but it doesn't seem to actually sink in with the masses when they do. The long-term conditioning causes the lies to become "common knowledge," and this makes it hard to get folks to believe the truth, even when those liars do fess up. What these times ARE about is all of US waking up to the truth of things and then to quit doing the disempowering things we do when we're in the dark about things. That's all that is required and yet that seems to be the scariest thing to most folks. The global happenings are really the least of it. How the psychological conditioning on society has impacted each individual's life seems to be the toughest part. Facing our own demons the scariest thing.

These people who "run" the world play a role, that, at a higher level, we asked them to play. They play the "adversary" (which is what "Satan" means). "They" are part of our Original Intent. It's all part of our human / earthly experience that we, at a higher level, chose to have. Yeppers, ultimately, we are all responsible for our own experiences.

The establishment basically offers us only one choice. It's through heavy influence and conditioning, not ultimate control, so we can still always choose something different. Just like Al Pacino, as the devil in the movie Devil's Advocate said, "Free will, ain't it a bitch?" And just like Pacino's character, the establishment can only "influence" us. If we choose to give authority of our lives, health and thinking to them, well, that's a personal choice and we've no one to blame but ourselves for the consequences. But it's oh so tough to play the victim when our predicament is of our own making, so people continue to point fingers, throw up their hands and say, "There's nothing I can do about it." Bunk. Yep, ain't Free Will fun? It's easy for us to get caught up in being the victim and speak of things "done unto" us, but much of what goes on in this world couldn't happen without our participation. All within our power to change... and powerful we are, indeed.

I worked with a Cambodian man once who was in his twenties in Cambodia during the Pol Pot / Khmer Rouge experience. He told me the people were so psychologically controlled that they could be tied to a fence with a wire-thin piece of string and they would make no attempt to get free. I looked my coworker in the eye and said, "Here in America we don't even need the piece of string." He said, "You're absolutely right."

The global elite also use the power of sacred symbology against us and also as a trademark of sorts, like a secret handshake that only those with "eyes to see and ears to hear" will understand. And yet "they" don't really truly understand this symbology either. They are coming from such a fearful, control-freak angle that they just don't get it. Jesus had told the establishment that they had the information, wouldn't let anyone else have it and yet they themselves didn't even know how to use it. I find that the establishment often uses it in exoteric ways. They make huge particle colliders and such rather than tapping into the "inner technology" (esoteric) that we all possess.

For more information on this sacred symbology, here are some researchers to look into. David Icke tends to expose the illusion at all levels - first he exposed the global control agenda, now he talks about the entire illusion of this whole realm. Michael Tsarion exposes the global elite also, and both David and Michael talk about how such things as sacred symbology are used against us. Both also speak of how to get our power back. William Henry, who calls himself a mythologist, tells how all that esoteric gnosis (knowledge), which "they" do their best to keep from us, could be put to use to be the empowered soul resurrection machines we were meant to be.

Yes, the huge control mechanism used by the establishment - "divide and conquer." This gets people focusing on differences in a disempowering way. We could celebrate diversity and still do better at seeing that we are more the same than different. We're all earth humans after all, all exposed to the same global control agenda, and all affected by the big debutant divide and conquer party we have come to know as the Tower of Babel episode.

As William Henry informs, Babel literally means "gate." Nimrod and his people wanted to tap into the same power that the "gods" had – the ability to open stargates in order to travel across distance, through time and between dimensions. They were putting together some rather high tech stuff, not just putting up some tall building. When the "gods" got wind of it, they divided the people, their language and culture to make it more difficult for them to work together. "They" are still using this tactic to this day. Perhaps it's high time we see who's really holding us down and it's not our fellow human, regardless of what culture, country, race, etc., that they belong to. It reminds me of a T-shirt I saw once. It plays on the old line of "We stand on the shoulders of giants."

> *I could probably actually get somewhere if I didn't have these giants standing on my shoulders. – T-shirt*

Then after we see that global control agenda, it still comes back to self. As I stated earlier, this "adversary" is of our own making at more than one level. If we can do it, we can undo it. If we can create a disempowered experience for ourselves, we can also create an empowered experience.

OUR PLANET, SOLAR SYSTEM, GALAXY, COSMOS

Our solar system may be part of a binary star system, meaning our own star Sol is not the only star involved here. This may be what accounts for the precession of the equinoxes. Precession has to do with our planet's axis pointing to different stars, or different points in space over time. It also accounts for the "age" we are in according to the zodiac. We are currently ending the age of Pisces and entering the Age of Aquarius.

The Great Year or Great Cycle of approximately 26,000 years will move us all the way around the twelve signs of the zodiac, with each age being a little over 2000 years. It was thought for centuries that this was due to the earth itself wobbling. But now Walter Cruttenden is saying that there is no evidence that our planet is wobbling in relation to local celestial bodies like the other planets in our solar system. That implies that the entire solar system is tilting over time.

Walter and his cohorts have contemplated the idea of a dark star of some sort that is difficult, if not impossible, to view, such as a brown dwarf, being our binary star. But now they are leaning towards thinking that our other star in this binary star system is Sirius. It's the brightest star in the sky (second brightest if you count our sun Sol as first brightest). Ancient cultures had many references to Sirius. The shaft in the Queen's Chamber in the Great Pyramid points to Sirius. What's significant about that is this - if we are not in a binary system with Sirius, then it, like all the other stars, should move over time. If the shaft in the Queen's Chamber always points to it, then that's a big clue that it is not moving relative to us. It's like it's on the other side of the merry-go-round from us and we move as a binary star system through the heavens. If Sirius is not our binary star, then that means that the ancient Egyptians designed the shaft in the Queen's chamber to point at Sirius now in our times and it wouldn't point there at other times.

It once was thought that multi-star systems were rare, but astrophysicists are finding that's not the case. Binary and other multi-star systems are the rule and not the exception. If our solar system is a single star system, it would be very rare and unique.

What's of most significance about the precession of the equinoxes and the possibility of a binary star system is that the Great Year cycle of 26,000 years would be like a much larger version of night and day. We would have the upper part of the sinusoidal oscillation lasting approximately 13,000 years and the lower part lasting another 13,000 years. And just like the light and

113

dark of our earth day and night, we would also have a much longer light and dark cycle due to the Great Year. We would have periods of enlightenment and wisdom and periods of forgetfulness and ignorance. Walter thinks the Dark Ages of our history would have been the very bottom of this oscillation and we are now slowly but surely climbing back out of that trough. We have been in very unenlightened times and have forgotten much that our ancient ancestors knew. So, this all implies that societal advancement is not linear as we've been led to believe. There are peaks and troughs, ebbs and flows. The ancients were more advanced than we are now.

In the last century, many ancient discoveries have been made. For example a "time piece" of sorts with very highly advanced gears and other workings from about 2000 to 4000 years ago was discovered. In more recent times this sophistication of gears was not used until the industrial age of the last few centuries. Even the idea of a heliocentric solar system, that we circle our sun and not the other way around, was known in ancient Greece about 2500 years ago, then forgotten, then rediscovered.

Other historical evidence of these peaks and troughs shows up in considering Mesopotamia or what we now know as Iraq. The highest level of ancient civilization there were the Sumerians. Instead of improving and advancing from there, it declined. It was then the Assyrians, Babylonians, then eventually to dust.

Walter Cruttenden speaks of how ancient cultures and the Andeans also "reversed" the use of words to do with past and future. Words we'd use for the future would have to do with the past in their languages and vice versa. This further reflects their understanding of these grand cosmic cycles and the polarity of energies through those cycles.

Freemasons, wiccans, pagans and others often refer to their art as the "craft". This body of knowledge they are utilizing is very ancient. William Henry quotes someone who I believe is a mason who jokes that CRAFT stands for Can't Remember A Friggin' Thing. We have forgotten much. Contrary to conventional thinking, we are NOT more advanced than the ancients. I don't know why even the pyramids themselves are not enough proof of this. We do not currently have the technology to build such structures. Why would we assume we're the best and brightest that have ever lived here?

These advance and decline cycles may be very cosmic and spiritual. In the up side of the cycle, we are literally being enlightened by cosmic rays or galactic core light and radiation or perhaps rays from another star system, like the Pleiades. Or another way to look at it would be that we are more conscious on the high side of this cycle. These rays cannot reach us as strongly when we are in the down side of the cycle. John Major Jenkins speaks of the ancient Mayan perspective on the Great Year / Cycle of precession. He says they didn't think of it as a circle so much as a breathing in and breathing out. We breathe in as we're coming into union with our cosmic heart and source and breathe out as we move away from it. He speaks of how winter solstice of the year 2012 marks the end of a period and the start of another where our winter solstice sun comes into union with the center of the Milky Way galaxy. William Henry's work contains information from ancient sources that may be telling us how to tap into, how to fully utilize the galactic core cosmic emissions to make an evolutionary leap. Those same emissions, or the cosmic dust they push at us, may be our very demise if we don't make some attempt to flow with these changing times and to transform ourselves. Dual meaning of Chaos - Crisis and Opportunity. Which do we choose?

Recently there is talk of our solar system being in another galaxy that is coming in at an angle to the Milky Way galaxy. This other galaxy is being absorbed into the Milky Way. This would account for why we can actually see the Milky Way. If we were on the same plane as it, would it appear across the heavens to us as it does? In my mind, this may also account for what it means for our sun to "align" with the galactic core.

Astrophysicist Paul LaViolette talks about these grand cycles and that there may be markers, beacons, literal warning signs, if you will, in our galaxy telling Milky Way galaxy inhabitants to be aware of when cosmic bursts are coming our way. He feels that the search for intelligent life elsewhere in the universe has missed the most obvious, biggest hint of that, which is the pulsars. Pulsars emit patterned frequencies that sometimes totally switch off, as if they were down for maintenance, only to come back on with their same pulse pattern. Some of them are placed in areas that would be likely to receive massive radiation if there were a galactic core burst, and those particular pulsars have a very visible twinkle, as if to say, "look here." And the signals span the spectrum to cover many frequencies so that no matter what "channel" a species were listening on, they would be very likely to get the signal. Just the kind of thing that should make SETI just ecstatic and yet this gets very little attention.

The Zodiac, its signs and glyphs also point to our galactic core. The glyphs of Sagittarius and Scorpio are the only glyphs containing arrows and they are signs adjacent to each other. In those constellations, their arrows, as seen from Earth's perspective point, to the Milky Way galactic core. The Zodiac has been talked about since ancient times. What were the ancients attempting to tell us? Check out Paul LaViolette's book and video Earth Under Fire for more details. The Seattle Metaphysical Library (www.seattlemetaphysicallibrary.org) can help you with this and much of what I mention in this book and far more.

The galactic core explosions appear as blue light. Many ancient cultures speak of the Blue Star. Cosmic rays will come directly from the galactic core and also through our sun. The current increased solar flare activity may offer evidence of this. Jay Weidner also addresses this and his personal journey that led to alchemical symbolism giving warning of such in his video *The Secrets of Alchemy* (www.jayweidner.com). Paul, Jay, and others speak of the double jeopardy involved when these comic rays come into our solar system. Not only do we take a direct hit by the cosmic rays, but the dust that comes with will coat our sun and cause it to heat up and go into constant, intense solar flare activity. This may explain the many accounts by ancient cultures of a great fire from the sky. Ancient texts and scientific evidence point to this type of event happening approximately 14,000 to 15,000 years ago.

There is much that many are not consciously aware of about our solar system. As I've mentioned already, the Caucasian race may very well have been from Mars originally. Being further from the sun, it would be make sense that a race on Mars would be lighter skinned than indigenous Earthlings. Ancient Druidic texts state such. Check into Michael Tsarion's work for more on this. Richard C. Hoagland thinks the monuments of Mars, which includes the

Face on Mars and other structures like pyramids there, are remnants of an ancient people.

Evidence points to the possibility that Mars was once the moon of a planet called Tiamat. Remnants of Tiamat are what we know as the asteroid belt, what the Sumerians called the hammered bracelet. Tiamat was a waterworld. Some say that it was here at the same time as Earth. Others say that Earth is part of the exploded Tiamat. There are various explanations for how Tiamat was destroyed. Some people point to advanced weaponry from visitors to the solar system being the cause of Tiamat's demise. Others think that perhaps an inbound comet, perhaps even Venus, which then fell into orbit around the sun. This may explain the Mayans fascination with tracking time based on Venusian cycles. Michael Tsarion's research of ancient texts indicates that Earth and Tiamat were here at the same time. This resonates with me. So, before Tiamat exploded, Earth was not as watery as it is today. Some of Tiamat's water hit Earth and this may be what the story of the deluge is about. I personally feel that Venus was part of Tiamat and that the comets were also. And this would still jive with those that think that Venus was once a comet. What we know as comets are chunks of ice and rock, which could very well be parts of an exploded planet. Comets have very long, elliptical orbits that take them way out to the outer reaches of the solar system and yet they still come back in close to the sun and the inner planets. If those comets formed at the same time as the solar system, why would they not have eventually found their way into a more circular orbit just as the planets have? But if they were from an exploding planet, from thousands of years ago, as opposed to million or billions of years ago when the solar system formed, then perhaps they would have such a strange orbit as they do.

Mike Hagen's radio show www.mikehagan.com, which has free archived radio interviews with Michael Tsarion, Jay Weidner, Walter Cruttenden, Paul LaViolette, Lewis Greenberg who talks about Immanuel Velikovsky's work, and many more can give you more details.

Obviously, the heads of NASA know something about our place in the cosmos and how astrology and ancient cultures point to this. As Richard C. Hoagland and others point out, NASA doesn't do much of anything without timing their actions with astrological /

astronomical alignments / relations and Egyptian mythology. Why in the world would a modern space program be so obsessed with such?

BEYOND 3D

Theoretical physicist, Dr. Michio Kaku, specializes in string field theory. He and others speak of other dimensions beyond the third dimension. He gives great, simple analogies for multiple dimensions and also for the concept of prophecy.

Fish in a pond may be rather unaware of anything beyond their pond. A person could pluck one fish out. Later, the person could throw the fish back into the pond and what stories he would have for his fellow fish. And they may not believe him, even though they saw him "disappear" and "reappear" right before their eyes. Many people have experienced the "beyond" in many ways and they too have a tough time getting their fellow humans to believe their reports. And yet in these times most especially, with the opportunities we have to evolve now, it's more important than ever for everyone to speak their own truth, to share their perspectives and to take in others' perspectives. And it's important that people don't allow their own experiences to be "vetoed" by the so-called experts. Too many times people will have an unusual experience and they let themselves be talked into denying the experience because the experts and society just "know" that's not possible.

Michio also uses the analogy of a person observing a bug crawling on the ground to explain prophecy. Being able to prophetize requires taking a "higher view", to rise up above the mundane to understand where we are heading. This can be done from a higher dimension. Michio proposes a bug crawling on the ground at a constant rate, perhaps in a sinusoidal pattern. He is in a two dimensional world. A person could look down on that bug, from a three dimensional world, observe its rate and pattern and be able to accurately predict where that bug will be in a minute, an hour or a day. In effect, the person is a prophet to the bug because he has the ability to predict the bug's future. But what can make the prophecy not happen is the bug's free will. He can change speed or direction any time he chooses.

Prophets could be seeing from a higher perspective, from a higher dimension, from a more "spiritual" dimension. They would be to us what the person was to that bug. And just like the bugs, we too could change direction at any time. This is why a prophecy heeded doesn't come true. If someone were blindfolded and started walking towards a cliff, someone else could serve as their "prophet" and warn them of their impending doom. If they heed the prophecy and change directions, then the prophecy no longer applies. Heeded prophecies don't come to be. Unheeded prophesies do. Y2K offers an example of a prophecy heeded, and henceforth, disaster avoided, at least for the most part. There were some interruptions, but, because people and companies took steps to remedy the problem, it created very few issues.

Sean David Morton is someone who uses remote viewing for making predictions and he is often very accurate. He is also very intuitive. But he is also just very knowledgeable of the true goings on in the world. He follows information that many people do not. He has been on radio programs making predictions and many times he says he's not using remote viewing or really even tapping into much intuition, he just pays attention to things that many people are unaware of. This demonstrates how just being awake and aware can also help us see potential futures that the next, less aware, person will not see.

If we continue down the path we're on, we'll get to where we are going.

I believe I can see the future
Because I repeat the same routine

Lyrics from "Every Day Is Exactly The Same" by Nine Inch Nails

But just like Michio's bug, we can change direction any time we choose and perhaps avert a potential future calamity. Learning about a higher perspective can help us change our present course and ,henceforth, our future. As Einstein said, "You can never solve a problem on the level on which it was created."

Richard C. Hoagland, who used to work for NASA and was Walter Cronkite's science advisor at a young age, has a theory of hyper-dimensional physics. He proposes that we influence and are influenced by other dimensions beyond those our five senses can detect. We can detect the effects of these other dimensional influences though. What many have termed "global warming" may very well be caused by what's happening in other dimensions. One clue is that other globes are also warming. Other planets and moons in our solar system are also heating up and it's happening from the inside out. Search online for Hoagland and his hyper-dimensional physics theory for more details.

Just as the planets have connections to other dimensions or have other parts of themselves in other dimensions, so do we. We can transmit and receive information back and forth from other levels of ourselves. We just need to re-learn this skill.

A QUANTUM EXISTANCE

To get a truer understanding of our existence, we could stand to see that there are different levels to everything. When we are able to flip from one level to another, we can see that seemingly contradictory things could actually all be true and at the same time. The different levels, or our perceptions of those levels, have different "rules." An example would be Newtonian physics vs. quantum physics.

Astrologer Rick Levine, in his video *Quantum Astrology*, talks about how the astrologers of years ago thought in Newtonian ways - cause and affect, which implies fate. In the same way, Newtonian scientists only understood the "particle" part of things and not the "wave" part. The astrologers of today, like the quantum scientists, can also understand the wave. Particle = fate, wave = free will. I tell people that astrological energies are an "influence," but we still have free will. How do we choose to handle the energetic influence? Will we re-act, as in act again, or will we re-spond, as in receiving energy, but transforming it into something different before sending it back out.

Quantum physicists have come to realize that the scientist's belief will affect the outcome of quantum experiments. They've been known to pull people off the street to conduct experiments for them because if the scientists themselves do it then the outcome follows their expectations. Joe Average off the street who knows next to nothing about quantum physics is less likely to have a bias about the outcome.

With humanity awakening to new possibilities through quantum physics, we are seeing we have much more influence ourselves over our reality. The first place we'll be able to affect is the energetic level. Until we learn to really use our consciousness, it will not have the same "big" affect on pool balls and planets as it does at the submicroscopic / energetic level.

TIME FOR THE TRUTH - WAKE UP DOROTHY

The obliteration of your isolation
The complete explosion
Of your fondest notion
This disintegration
Is your elevation
It's a grand illusion, it's a grand illusion

You're crying, you're trying so hard now
You'll be laughing
A hundred thousand years
There is only one day
And tonight is the night
It's a grand illusion

The devastation of your separation,
The disillusion of
Your constitution,
It's exhilaration, it's your liberation
It's a grand illusion, it's a grand illusion

Lyrics from "Grand Illusion" by Joan Osborne

A grand illusion that it's high time we wake up to. We've had many experiences, many adventures in our sleepy slumber, but it's time for something new. As I'd written earlier, if we knew the truth, our choices would change. And once you learn the truth, you can't unlearn it, now you have to own it. But, the truth shall set us free. I have been amazed with how much learning the truth of the world and accepting my own power has provided me with freedom. And even as the intensity of these awesome times increases, just understanding what these times are about, knowing who we all truly are, the more of Life's mysteries I know, the freer and less burdened I feel. And what a wonderful feeling that is.

We are at the end of an age and other cycles, including the Great Cycle of the Precession of the Equinoxes. In order to move on to the next age, the truth of the old one must be revealed - like it or lump it. Even those behind the global control agenda will assist in these truths finally surfacing because "they" can't move on either if not, and they know it. I read something online somewhere that really nailed what needs to happen here. It had to do with the whole "extra terrestrial" thing. Like I said earlier, these times are not about forcing the government to reveal / admit what they know, it's about seeking the truth for ourselves. So, that's why the whole Disclosure Project - about just that, forcing the government to fess up to what they know about ETs - is yet another diversion, a distraction. The onus of the truth is on each of us. You want to know the truth? Then go seek it. Don't expect it to be handed to you or others on a silver platter, most especially by those who deceived you in the first place.

Some of you may have been noticing numbers come up repeatedly. Perhaps you see them on clocks, license plates and elsewhere. They have meaning. This is one of many ways that the Universe is attempting to communicate with you. Numerology or angel numeric messages as defined by Doreen Virtue and others can help you make the translation.

One number that many see is 11:11. One meaning for this is "enlightenment." I feel that enlightenment is certainly the end goal, but, oftentimes when we are shown 11:11 it's at a time when we are having an experience which we don't know why we are having it, we don't know what it means. A clearer meaning for 11:11 is "the initiate." You see 11:11 because you are being put through an initiation.

In ancient times, there were mystery schools in the world. There are a few around now also. These schools put people through initiations, which use symbology to teach. The meaning of these symbolic initiations is not given to the initiate. Like I said, it's not being handed to us on a silver platter, we must have the desire to question, to seek, to know. The meaning for the initiate is for them to find out on their own, in their own time, in their own way.

Freemasons, other organizations and religions also provide these same kinds of initiations, sometimes by announcing it is an initiation, sometimes not. But one need not run off and join one of these schools or organizations because Life itself is providing the initiatory process. Just show up on Earth and the process begins. Regardless of how these initiations are delivered, it's God / Source / the Divine / your higher-self prompting you to question and to seek the answers to your questions. You're being offered the opportunity to "catch the spark."

There's a part of even the most unaware of people that knows that Power and Responsibility go hand in hand. And many have been so conditioned to not take responsibility that they will willingly give away their power. It's the "there's nothing I can do about it" mentality. Each and every one of us is potentially a very powerful being, gods and goddesses - if we'd only quit telling ourselves otherwise. It's high time we got out of our own way.

And the first part of taking responsibility and, henceforth, reclaiming our power is to raise our awareness about the REAL current state of things here on Earth. Not only will we need to learn about our outer environment here (ecological, political, food, medicine, media, etc.), but also, more significantly, it will serve us to go inward, to get back in touch with our own inner environment. And, the "out there" is a reflection of the "in here."

"Your vision will become clear only when you look into your heart. Who looks outside, dreams. Who looks inside, awakens." - Carl Jung

It's time to study REAL history as opposed to the lies we've been slathered in. More and more people are coming to understand the truth about our past and the significance of our times. We stand on the shoulders of giants. Many brave souls down through history have faced torture, ruin, persecution and death in order to keep the truth in this world so that we can come upon their work in these times and awaken. It's not about the truth being handed to us. It's about each and every one of us making our own personal "Grail Quest", our quest for knowledge and wisdom.

Michael Tsarion says that folks often ask him why he's so into history. He says he's really not. He just wants to know why things are in the state they're in now and that requires researching REAL history (or herstory in many cases). I so can relate. I used to read a lot of sci-fi books, but, since getting into my "truth seeking," I have read very few works of fiction (although much "fiction" comes from very inspired, in-spirit, authors). Our own human story is SO fascinating, even compared to fiction where the author can take creative license. Whether we realize it or not though, we gods and goddesses are also taking creative license in everything we do. On top of that, the truer version of history one uncovers is just so empowering. The energies of these times are calling all this forth. Urging for the personal quest. Even our leaders who do care to help bring the truth out cannot "save" us. We must save ourselves. And as the line goes - If the people will lead, the leaders will follow.

And they say that a hero can save us.
I'm not gonna stand here and wait.
I'll hold onto the wings of the eagles.
Watch as we all fly away.

Lyrics from "Hero" by Chad Kroeger (from the Spiderman soundtrack)

Change can happen in a moment, a heartbeat, a breath. But like a good friend of mine finishes with, "… but resistance can last forever." Let's stop resisting and get out of our own way. The Universe is handing us a grand opportunity to shatter the grand illusion.

You're out of the woods
You're out of the dark
You're out of the night
Step into the sun, step into the light

Keep straight ahead
For the most glorious place
On the Face of the Earth
Or the sky

Hold onto your breath
Hold onto your heart

Hold onto your hope
March up to the gate
And bid it open

Lyrics from "Optimistic Voices" from The Wizard of Oz

TAKING RESPONSIBILITY & ACCEPTING POWER

In the "old system" that is on its way out, irresponsibility has been encouraged. Why? Because power and responsibility go hand in hand. We've often heard it expressed this way – with great power comes great responsibility. But reversing that is also significant – surrendering responsibility surrenders power.

Dr. Lorraine Day gave a simple example of how being irresponsible is encouraged these days. One can go to a department store, buy a dress, wear it once and return it, no questions asked. Sounds like the cheapest dress rental available. Allstate tells me my next accident will be forgiven. How's about forgiving me on insurance because I haven't had any accidents. What a concept. Budweiser delivery trucks have bumper stickers that say Beeresponsible. Read that again. They know what they are saying. Hmm. It'd be interesting to take that up with the ATF since there are laws against subliminal messaging in the beer industry. I can't imagine a worse message for a beer (use that term loosely in Bud's case) manufacturer than "be irresponsible."

It's high time we take responsibility of our lives and start tapping into our own Christ Consciousness.

One of Nostradamus' quatrains speaks of the King of Terror. He was not the only one to speak of such. The King of Terror is often associated with Jesus H. Christ and his various incarnations and the return of Christ Consciousness to the world. Why would Christs and Christ Consciousness be associated with terror? Well, it's all about Truth, Power and Responsibility. We've been sold a lie, and worse yet, we bought it. We've been slathered in disempowering information since the word "go" however many thousands of years ago since the beginning of what we consider "modern man." We've been made to believe that we are not the gods and goddesses that we truly are. When the truth comes along, when a new enlightening, empowering message returns to the world, like it is now, people can become literally terrified by realization of how we

125

did buy the lie. Then the prospects of their own ensuing personal power can also become terrifying. Ah, yes, with power comes responsibility, and part of us knows that. It's been all too convenient in our collective on-going trauma to say the dysfunctional state of things, including our own very personal life, health and state of being, is beyond our power to change. Not so. Best not be if we'd like to see Earth's human race continue to exist. We are presently being challenged with the choice of extinction or evolution. As traumatizing as the shattering of one's belief system can be, the truth shall set you free. The truth is that we are very powerful beings.

> *Our worst fear is not that we are inadequate, our deepest fear is that we are powerful beyond measure. It is our light, not our darkness that most frightens us. We ask ourselves, 'who am I to be so brilliant, gorgeous, talented and fabulous?' Actually, who are we not to be? You are a child of God: Your playing small doesn't serve the world. There is nothing enlightening about shrinking so that other people won't feel insecure around you. We were born to make manifest the glory of God within us. It is not just in some of us, it is in everyone and as we let our own light shine we unconsciously give other people permission to do the same. As we are liberated from our own fear, our presence automatically liberates others.*

> *~Marianne Williamson*

Jesus H. Christ said, "Have I not said ye are gods? You too shall do these and greater things." When we get in trouble is when we deny our own power. The reason why lawyers are thriving these days is because people don't want to take responsibility. A part of us knows that Power and Responsibility (the ability to respond) go hand in hand. In order to deny our responsibility, we have to first deny our own power. But that doesn't mean that we stop creating. We are constantly creating. By denying our power, denying the fact that we are gods and goddesses, we end up creating the very things we don't want.

> *We shake our fists and say,*
> *"Well good golly we're mad*
> *That God kills children with our very own hands"*

126

We claim innocence and not to understand
But do we, do we?

Lyrics from "Do You" by Jewel.

How many times have you heard someone say, "There's nothing I can do. It's just little ol' me. I can't affect the world. " And yet we do. And when people say such, it may not be in relation to huge world problems, but for their very own lives. They put their spiritual lives in the hands of their clergy. They let the priest, pastor, minister determine what they will consider spiritually. They sit in their pews for an hour a week to get their download on topics of someone else's choosing and the other 167 hours per week it doesn't even occur to them to seek more. They put their minds in the hands of the education system and the media and, here again, never consider a personal quest for answers, but let the information be delivered to them on a silver platter. Never mind that silver platter delivers a whole heap of disempowering propaganda. They put their health in the hands of their grocer, doctor and the FDA. They claim they have no time for these very personal things and say that's up to the "experts." They give responsibility, power and authority of their own lives over to someone else then get angry when everything falls apart. They lose their connection to both spirit and Mother Earth. They dis their own bodies and have the audacity to scratch their heads when they develop chronic illness.

In the book *Blink,* Malcolm Gladwell talked about military strategists, stock exchangers and then improv comedy troupes. Bottom line, "spontaneity isn't random." All these folks know their line of work well and study, experience, rehearse, etc., but they really make their living by making split second decisions when it counts the most. They know that in that moment all the planning in the world just isn't realistic.

Malcolm writes that the founder of an improv theater said this:

If you'll stop reading for a moment and think of something
you wouldn't want to happen to you, or to someone you
love, then you'll have a thought of something worth
staging or filming. We don't want to walk into a restaurant
and be hit in the face by a custard pie, and we don't want
to suddenly glimpse Granny's wheelchair racing towards
the edge of a cliff, but we'll pay money to attend

127

enactments of such events. **In life, most of us are highly skilled at suppressing action.** *All the improvisation teacher has to do is reverse this skill and he creates 'gifted' improvisers.* **Bad improvisers block action, often with a high degree of skill. Good improvisers develop action.** *(My emphasis.)*

How profound. Evil prevails when good men fail to act. Again... responsibility - the ability to respond.

I see this exact potential in everyday life for everyone. We prepare ourselves by seeking and learning. We can set our intent for end goals, allow the Universe to fill in the how, the details of getting there, but we too do our part along the way. But what is our part? If we listen, we'll be guided each step of the way. If we pay attention, we can respond as situations arise. But since we can't read the future, we don't know what will arise until it does. We have to improvise, but can do so from a prepared place, just as these groups spoken of in *Blink.* That preparation came about by being present in the moments leading up to this moment. One moment prepares us for the next. We can listen to our inner guidance in that moment rather than thinking we can plan everything out ahead of time.

On the spiritual path, as we come from a place of mind and body, we start to prepare at those levels. Our experiences, lessons and the information we seek help to provide that preparation. As we get more in touch with our emotions and allow them expression, we connect more to spirit, to our higher selves. As we hear ourselves say to God, "Thy will be mine", we start to turn ourselves over, surrendering to our higher selves. The closer we get to that, the more present we are. When that connection has been made to a certain level, we just trust and flow along with each step of guidance that our higher selves provide. We stop planning and live spontaneously according to the agenda set by our higher selves. The planning is done at a higher level. The Divine works hard so we don't have to.

Take responsibility. Keep authority over your life - YOUR life, not anyone else's. There could be a definite sense of relief just from this alone. You can lay down that unnecessary burden of others' issues, problems, choices. It's not your burden and you really don't have much power there anyway and why should you? It's not your life to live. It's theirs.

> *To take on another's tests under your name is cosmic cheating and will incur karma for all concerned.*

> *A few years ago I heard a mystic say that the creed for the new world must be "We are all one, and I am responsible for you." And a friend of mine once said that the ancient meaning of Christ is "to give what is needed." Now we can understand the significance of "responsibility" – the quality of being responsible without meddling so that we can focus on giving that which is needed. But all we really have to give is our consciousness, which means that once again the starting point in any right and loving relationship is the individual you see in the mirror.*

> *From "The Angels Within Us" by John Randolph Price*

Letting go of wanting to control others' experiences and lessons frees you up to put your focus where it will do the most good, make the greatest impact – on your own life, issues, choices, healing. And isn't that what's most important? Who doesn't understand that one person can't do it all? So, then wouldn't it make sense to get the biggest bang for your buck, so to speak? Put your focus, intent and efforts where it WILL do the most good.

> *"Am I getting involved with these people for the right reason?"*
> *"What are your reasons?"*
> *"I made mistakes... I'd like to use my talents, my gifts to correct things."*
> *"If you want to change the world, first change yourself. Then your part in changing the world is finished."*
> *"I don't think I'm there yet."*
> *"It's a monumental task, changing oneself. You need to become more self-centered."*
> *"I'm pretty selfish as it is."*
> *"Not selfish. Focused on self. One's aim should be to know oneself truly apart from one's place in the world."*

> *Dialogue from the TV series Damages.*

No one can take authority over our lives, but we sure can give it away. No one else can or will take care of you the way you can take care of yourself and it's not their responsibility to do so anyway. You have ultimate responsibility over your own life. And the next person has responsibility over theirs. Take the responsibility that is yours and, in so doing, tap into the power that is you.

EXPERIENTIAL REALM MEET INFINITE CONSCIOUSNESS

Again, despair.com offers some tongue in cheek wisdom. "Fear - Until you have the courage to lose sight of the shore, you will not know the terror of being forever lost at sea."

We came here to experience these things, which can't be experienced in "God's realm". We came here to feel things we cannot feel in "Heaven." Heaven can be right here on Earth, but we ultimately came here to experience Hell also, something we cannot experience in "God's realm."

People get caught up in assigning good and bad labels to emotions and experiences. It is what it is. Our higher selves want to have these experiences and have them they will, albeit through their mundane counterparts - us. Perhaps we could let go of judgment and just allow the experiences we came here to have. Rather than fighting the upwelling of so-called "negative" emotions, we could sit in them, roll in them like a dog would roll in something stinky. It's like a genre of music or an art form that isn't necessarily to your liking, but you can certainly appreciate the artistry in it, "Isn't this just exquisite suckage?!" And you are the artist. If you're gonna do it, do it right. Experience it fully.

Now, having said that - why not apply it also to Joy, Bliss, Love, Peace, Happiness, Contentment. I've too often seen these feelings unnerve folks. There have been times when I have cleared and released enough outdated beliefs, put down enough baggage and burdens to feel new levels of Joy, Peace, and Contentment that really had nothing to do with anything going on "out there." It was about inner burdens shed. At those times, I too felt how unnerving Joy could be when one is not used to it. I did manage to push through and allow it.

These emotions have become foreign to many of us. Some people will literally sabotage their own happiness, contentment, etc., because they just aren't used to it. They'd rather stay with the familiar and camp out in a very uncomfortable comfort zone. I have also experienced times when I was given a heads up on new paths and directions for myself due to the inner work I'd done and could feel what I can only describe as a freight train of Joy coming barreling down at me. I knew there may be a little more clearing and releasing and that certain things would need to fall into place first, but I could feel the energy of Joy approaching hard and fast. I've bawled my eyes out knowing that I was about to step into new levels of Joy and Happiness, wondering if I had what it took to accept it when it did arrive, pushing through those feelings to continue the work of clearing and releasing to make sure there were no blockages to receiving that Joy. One other dysfunction in this passing Age of Pisces has been that people don't feel worthy of feeling these awesome things. When you do experience those emotions, I'd advise the same - sit in it, roll in it, soak it up - "What exquisite Peace this is!" etc.

This is ultimately about being present, regardless of what is presented. If you would like to know more about being present, look into Eckhart Tolle's work. He's the "Power of Now" guy. Wonderful message he puts out. Indeed. It would serve each of us, and our planet, for us to deal with what is right in front of us in every moment rather than stew over a past that is gone and fret over a future that may never be. ("Don't cry, it might never happen.") And being present not only implies right now, but also right here. Again, deal with what is right in front of you. Sit in it. Even if it's something that we might judgmentally / relatively label as unpleasant, just sit in it. It's what is being "presented" to you.

"Today is a gift - which is why they call it the present." -
Bill Keane

A friend of mine was going through a tough period of time, work was chaotic, she was in the middle of a breakup with a lover and her father was passing. In the middle of this, I was talking to her on the phone and she said she was being very present and didn't want to miss any of it, to get cheated out of any of what she was experiencing. It made me smile to hear her say this, since at one time, she was one to "tune out" when faced with challenges.

The multiple layers of our existence are like peeling an onion, we just keep uncovering new aspects, new perspectives. At a mundane level, we can be down in the muck and mire and not see past the end of our noses. Then we can pull up far enough to see the control and manipulation by those at the top of institutions and organizations. You can pull up above that and see that the reason why they attempt to control us is because they operate in a state of fear and they know our potential power, know us better than we know ourselves and they fear us. You rise up even further and you see that we co-created the controllers, the manipulators as part of our original intent for this experiential realm. We are all responsible for our own existence. And God has ultimate responsibility for it all. So if you must place blame, take it to God. He / She / It prefers it that way. He'd rather see you take it out on Him than get caught up in the "adversary's" divide and rule tactic and be loose cannons in the world pointing the finger of blame at your fellow human. You'll eventually forgive God also, but this route creates a little less chaos here on Earth. And keep in mind that forgiveness is ultimately for the forgiver, not the forgiven. You set yourself free by forgiving.

There is often reference to this realm being a "classroom" or "school." David Icke, in his book *Infinite Love is All There Is, Everything Else is Illusion*, says it's silly to think that beings who know all have anything to learn. He's absolutely right, but we did not create this realm and come here to know everything, we're here to *experience* everything. I'll reference Neale Donald Walsch's Conversations With God book series for a rebuttal on David's point. In "God's Realm" we're in the absolute - light, positive and all knowing. But we wanted to not only know all, but to experience all. So in this experiential realm, we can choose to step outside ourselves and then look back upon ourselves. We can experience what is not us - darkness, negative and ignorance.

Now, don't get me wrong, I'm aware of what David is presenting and am not in conflict with it. He's just saying that we need not buy into this illusion (of our own creation) anymore. We can connect to consciousness and no longer get swept up into "the matrix," but I guess it depends on what level of perspective you are looking at this from. If these illusory experiences were not something we wanted, we wouldn't be here. There is no "have to" to this. It's more like "choose to." And yet just like we chose to co-create this illusion, we can all choose to step out of it, or at least step out of the illusion of it. And it may be high time that we do start to step out of our illusory experiences. And why not? We've about exhausted this level of experience anyway. We're just repeating the same ol', same ol'.

There are so many different levels of perspective. If we can easily flip between all, perhaps we can have the "and / both" (all) that I spoke of earlier. Why not be aware of the illusion and yet still grounded into it - in the world and not of it. The "Land of Oz" that we live in is SO beautimous, far more colorful than our home in "Kansas" (Heaven). We strive to return home, but how's about we truly be the connection between Heaven and Earth and have both. Why can't Dorothy be in the dream and still be wide-awake. Like Pat Benatar's song lyrics "Wide awake in dreamland." Those who study ancient texts say our ancestors experienced just this. They knew that they were here for experiences and yet still knew who they truly were.

I get the distinct impression that being at this dense of a level of existence is still fairly rare. We may look to beings in higher / less dense levels as being somehow more advanced than us, but are they really? They may have the advantage over us of not wearing a veil, so they are more aware of the various levels, but could they do what we do here? We often think of this dense physicality as being very limiting, but I've known folks who talk to higher-level entities who have to admit they just can't tell certain things about our existence from their perspective. Some may not have the experience with this perspective that we do either. I've gotten the impression that God and our individual souls have worked our way "down" into more and more dense levels until we got to the three dimensional realm we've been in here. Like I said, perhaps not every being has had the privilege of experiencing this level of density.

The Hopi have said that, in these present times, we will move from the 3rd World, quickly through the 4th World into the 5th World. You could perhaps replace the word World with Dimension or Density. The entities that David Icke speaks of controlling us have been doing so from the 4th density. From our old 3rd density perspective, the 4th density is our emotions. And yes, indeed, we have been controlled through Fear. I am very firmly convinced from personal experience and observation of the happenings on this

133

planet that we entered the 4th density with the eclipse of August 1999. My life has changed so very significantly since that time. Before then, if you had told me I'd go through all I've been through since, I probably never would have believed you. I would think some of you know the feeling. And this world has gone through so very much since then also. We can think of the 4th density as Hell, as we cross the cathartic Lake of Fire on our way to the bottom layer of Heaven, the 5th density. Like I've said, the road to Heaven goes through Hell.

But now... let's have it all – Heaven and Earth together.

ON THE PATH TO HEALING

One day I drove by a business called Personality Cleaners. I laughed and thought, "By God, there's a lot of folks who could use that service."

As I said before, at a higher level, we contracted with other souls to activate wounds. When our wounds, experiences, our want for love and affection have made us over-compromise and our modes of "defense" have moved us so far away from our true selves that the pain becomes unbearable, we must knuckle down to the work of healing and returning to our true selves. It need not all be so much "work" though. The choice is ours. We can go voluntarily or kicking and screaming. If Life wants to bring healing and transformation gently, then allow it, receive it. The pain we experience has to do with resisting the healing. Less resistance, less pain. If Life insists on you going from point A to point B, then go you shall. If you dig your heels in along the way, you'll just rip yourself up. The Hopi elders put out a message a few years back about how to survive and thrive through these chaotic times we are in. They advised to not cling to the riverbank of the old ways and instead push off into the middle of the stream, push off into the current. It may be a bumpy ride, but it's better to flow along with that changing river than to be dashed against the rocks on the bank.

We've also contracted with other souls here to help heal our wounds. It's all part of this human / earthly experience that we chose to have. Many folks think the next person is not wise enough to teach them anything. If they themselves were a good student, they could learn even from those people who may not even be as evolved as they are... or that they think they are. Don't wait for a teacher who walks on water. By the time they do, it may be too late for you. We're all coming up through this together.

I do healing work with people. For those familiar with Hindu mythology, the kind of energy I bring is like Kali energy. Oftentimes, especially from westerners, this is defined as destructive, which is one way that God works through us G.O.D. = Generator Operator Destroyer. A better word might be de-constructive, for nothing is ever truly destroyed, but is instead transformed. The old ways of being, believing, thinking, emoting must be torn down to make way for the new, shattering the old to free us from the prison of our own outdated belief systems. Like the analogy Phillip Mountrose used about Emotional Freedom Technique (EFT), when remodeling a room, haul out the old stuff before bringing in the new. Break down to break through.

In the preface of her book *Magdalene's Lost Legacy*, Margaret Starbird tells of a dream her friend had: People were traveling through the desert with camels that were very loaded down with baggage. They ran out of water. They drove the camels as hard as they could but eventually the camels collapsed in a heap. After awaking and thinking about her dream, Margaret's friend felt that the reasonable thing for her dream characters to do was to unload the baggage and ride the camels out of the desert. Margaret goes on to say that we, like the dream characters, are attempting to carry too much old baggage and that will result in our demise. In order to survive and to continue on our journey, we must put down the burdens of old beliefs that no longer have any place in our experiences.

St. Augustine said, "Lord, I pray not for a lighter load, but for stronger shoulders." Well, I guess it depends on what "load" you're talking about. I would gladly take on more load concerning the work of energetically helping this planet and her inhabitants to heal and raise their frequency. But if we're talking about a load of crap, a load of useless baggage that is just weighing us down, that is adding to ours and the world's problems, well, hey, let's shed that load already, eh? Let's become more "enlightened", not just more luminous, but lighter, as in less heavy. Time to lay down our unnecessary burdens.

When I'm doing healing work, there are times I literally feel like an exorcist. I heard a radio interview once with a Lutheran exorcist. Yep, he absolutely does what I do. He's just using different terminology to explain it, but it's the same thing. He talks of driving out one's demons, I talk about balancing emotional energy and clearing blockages. He finally just flat said that it's emotions. The "demons" may be passed from one generation to the next. This explains so-called "curses" put on families. If one person is wounded and doesn't get to the business of healing (in many cases they've not known how), they pass on their woundedness to the next generation. The person who is molested as a child will, as an adult, often go on to do the same thing to children.

But it doesn't even have to be a case of physical or sexual abuse. The global elite know that if they can manage to get one generation of people to believe something that is disempowering and self-sabotaging, then those people "lovingly", albeit unknowingly, pass that along to the next generation. So we've gotten to a state where even those who love us - parents, teachers, preachers, etc., are telling us untruths and disempowering us, and in their own highly conditioned state of being, they have no idea what they are doing. "Forgive them Father, they know not what they do." Somewhere along the line, we have to be courageous enough to say, "The buck stops here", to address our own healing so we don't then become the abusers ourselves, so that we don't, in turn, wound and brainwash the next generation.

I knew a young woman that thinks her grandmother has some very backward thinking, as her grandmother says she is living in sin for living with a man that she's not married to. Then this same woman tells me at a later date that if she had a son and he had a friend that had gay parents then she wouldn't allow her son to stay at his friend's house. On top of this, this woman herself is bisexual (at least, if not just flat lesbian by her own admission) and yet "due to her belief system," (her words) she cannot exercise the same-gender side of her sexuality because it's "wrong." She's been there, done that and when she's gone there she was "wrong" in her mind. Now it's one thing to deny oneself, but she's already planning on how to run her unborn offspring's lives. And she herself is very independent. God forbid anyone tell her how to live, even if it is her grandmother. And this is just her speaking of the hypothetical situation of her potential son's friend having gay parents. What if the boy's friend was gay? What if her son himself is gay? And so the conditioning, the self-sabotaging belief system, the control gets passed on to the next generation. As Brenda Russell sings about, "When will we all catch on?"

As I said under Demonization of the Occult, homosexuals were one of many groups persecuted by Hitler. Whether he understood it or not, there was major power in homosexuality since it allows for the power of sex while removing the consequence of conceiving unwanted children. Barbara Marciniak's books, containing her channelings of the Pleiadians, tell of how our intentional energy can be utilized to not create unwanted pregnancies. Wouldn't that be nice, if for no other reason that to end the rhetoric about abortion in government so our so-called leaders could actually get something done?

The Bible speaks of Jesus driving out 7 demons from Mary Magdalen. In *The Magdalen Manuscripts*, Mary tells us, through channel Tom Kenyon, that Jesus just did a chakra clearing on her. Energy healing like Reiki, Emotional Freedom Technique (EFT) and a myriad of other modalities get rid of emotional blockages just like the chakra clearing (demon expulsion) that Jesus did for Mary.

I am a Reiki "healer". This is actually a misnomer, as the only one who can heal someone is themselves, but I and others like me channel healing life-force energy to folks to help them with their healing work. Before working with someone, I ask if they have ever done energy healing work. I explain to them that it is not like waving a magic wand and magically all their problems go away. Quite to the contrary. Initially it may feel like things have gotten worse. In order to heal, we must first know what to heal, what to work on.

The alchemists talk of turning lead into gold. This is more symbology, not to be taken literally, although a master alchemist may very well be able to do just that. What this means is re-turning an "ordinary" human (lead) into the god or goddess (gold) they truly are. The alchemists use the analogy of melting metal. The fire provides the catalyst, then the dross or impurities rise to the top so that they may be skimmed off and only the pure metal remains. The same is true of the healing process. Healing energy work helps to draw our "dross" to the surface so that we can clear and release it.

Emotionally, it often feels like we are re-living what caused the wound in the first place. Re-mind yourself that it only feels that way and you are safe, you're not re-experiencing it, you're just allowing the old emotions to surface so they can be released, again, lightening your load. And to throw in some symbology that I have observed applies to this... on the third day, you'll rise again. Often after doing energy work, I've observed that people's "dross" rises to the surface in the first 3 to 4 days. If you're around them, best dodge the arrows.

I caught part of a TV evangelist's sermon one day. He was speaking of fear and how damaging and debilitating it is. He, of course, used the Bible to back up his message. He said there is a verse in Matthew about who would not make it to the Kingdom of Heaven. He gave the analogy of the ingredient list on foods. What there's the most of is what's listed first, then on down the line. Well, on this list in Matthew, of those who would not make it to the Kingdom of Heaven, were, of course, murderers and thieves and the like, but at the top of the list was the fearful. One of the greatest opportunities these present times are offering us is to transcend our fears, to face them head-on, to have the courage to think, do, act and live even when we're scared, to allow our fears to surface and then release them.

It's that simple wisdom of Love is the answer. Love is a high frequency vibration with a short wavelength. Fear is a low frequency vibration with a long wavelength. Love, henceforth, is more powerful, more influential as it's frequency will "cross" or intersect our personal vibration more times than fear will. Nevertheless, the human race has been conditioned over a long period of time to be VERY fearful. Fear has gotten to be it's own entity, influencing all facets of our lives. And yet if we can summon up the courage to step out of Fear, then the effects of Love will snowball in a hurry. Only the pure of heart can cross the Lake of Fire. Egyptians made depictions of a human heart on a scale being weighed against a feather. Only those with a heart as light as a feather can cross to the Kingdom of Heaven.

Like Tracy Chapman sings about, the map to the labyrinth is within us. We already know everything there is to know. We have all the answers. We just have a consciousness veil that, perhaps at this point in time we could stand to tear away so we can reconnect to all knowingness. Outside information can provide us with esoteric information, ancient wisdom, the mysteries of life, providing some clues, some stimulus that will help us re-member, to tap into that map within us.

> *Each reader reads only what is within himself. The book is only a sort of optical instrument, which the writer offers to the reader to enable the latter to discover in himself what he would not have found but for the aid of the book.*

From "The Past Recaptured" by Marcel Proust

Look, feel, know, listen for resonance. And right there are the clues to your "clairs" respectively – clairvoyance, clairsentience, claircognizance, clairaudience. Which words do you hear yourself using to indicate your strongest clair? "I *see* what you mean." "I *feel* ya." "I *know* where you're coming from." "I *hear* what you're saying."

> *Darling are you feeling*
> *The same thing that I'm seeing*

Lyrics from "The Saddest Song I've Got" by Annie Lennox

What I have found signals resonance is a strong emotional response. Those emotions run the gamut. It may be an "ah ha" moment, or a feeling of love, warmth, peace, but it may also be intense denial, anger, frustration, hatred, the desire to "kill the messenger." The information is obviously resonating with you at some level if you have this strong response.

It's important that we hone our discernment skills. We practice this by exposing ourselves to a variety of information and perspectives. There are plenty of information sources that are really about disinformation, and yet disinformation depends heavily on the truth in order to sell you a lie. So, there is much to be gleaned even from listening to disinformation specialists. But yes, it will require you kick in your discernment skills. And even when hearing from folks who have no conscious intention of deceiving you, you still have to use your own discernment. They may be very conditioned themselves and don't know that they are uttering untruths to you. And, regardless, their truth may not be yours. They may be speaking of something that works for them, but not for you.

If you look up discernment in the dictionary, you will often see that the word judgment is used to define it and vice versa, and yet I've always felt there was a slight difference between the two. The best definition I've heard yet comes from Patricia Leva who wrote *Traveling the Interstate of Consciousness*. She said, and I paraphrase, that Judgment is a left-brained logical function based in reason and Discernment is a right-brained intuitive function based in knowingness.

Judgment also means balance, like Lady Justice holding the scales, like the Justice / Balance card in Tarot. Lady Justice judges blindly. She just knows the rules of balance and balance must be maintained. Judgment Day is not about being condemned, most especially by God. It's more about being "judged" by the "rules" of balance in this realm that we co-created for our experiences. It's about what goes around, comes around, what we put out comes back to us. John Randolph Price in *The Angels Within Us* said that Jesus and Paul taught about cause and effect, action and reaction, compensation, and karma. What we sow we reap. What's most significant about this is what our beliefs are, for that's what Life will mirror back to us. We may not harm anyone, and yet still have harm come to us because we believe it will.

> *The truth is, we really do not know what we believe until we see the effects in the outer world. We say that we believe in harmony, goodwill, and right relations, but perhaps we are more certain of a hostile world, a competitive jungle, and obstructive forces. It is the latter that will be impressed on the sensitive karmic plates, producing personal conflict, opposition, and bondage – and all this will continue until the beliefs are changed.*

The balance of this realm must be restored or we will create our own demise. No one else is judging us, we judge ourselves. We will face the consequences of our choices. These are the rules of the game that we set up for ourselves here.

The character of Jesus H. Christ used parables, and through metaphors brought in the right-brain and intuition, not just logic and reason, so we can bring both brain hemispheres into play and achieve balance and wholeness. The left-brain involves masculine energy and the right-brain involves feminine energy. Jesus knew what he was doing by using parable and metaphor to bring back feminine energy for balance in an unbalanced patriarchal society.

Get in touch with God / the Divine / Source / the One / your higher self, whatever you choose to call it. Start the dialogue. Perhaps you won't hear the answers right away, but at least put the questions out. In the process, you are acknowledging your words are being heard. You're speaking to someone inside you, not outside. The connection is always there, we just get so caught up in the drama of this realm we forget about that Divine connection. Eventually, you'll hear the answers coming. Initially, Life will be doing everything it can to reach you in whatever way that works. Pay attention. We just need to be awake and aware enough to catch the communications, to see the synchronicities. But, yes, eventually, it will be an ongoing dialogue in your head and heart. And don't worry about all the brainwashed souls who are going to think you're crazy because you "hear voices". When we are unsane is when we DON'T hear our inner voice, when all we can acknowledge is the illusion and miss the reality of Joy, Love, Peace, and our own Power.

In the section Our Beliefs as Our Environment, I said to "Learn from the parts of your life that ARE working." Here's one example of this from my personal life. When I do Reiki with someone, I know that the healing is going on between the person and the Divine. I am just there as a channel, a facilitator, a liaison, a translator. I have always felt like this when doing Reiki and I do my best to just "get out of the way." By taking this stance I am giving myself over to Divine guidance. I let go, let God. I let the Divine call the shots. What I say and do to and with this person who is being healed is what the Divine is guiding me to do. Ok, that's an area of my life that works. I see the results from that.

I observed how well that worked and applied it to my own life. If I can "get out of the way" to help someone else, I can do that to help myself also. John Randolph Price in his book *The Angels Within Us* equates it to a clarinet that thinks it can play itself:

> *It has free will, which means that it thinks it can play itself,*
> *so it functions in the world by striking its own keys,*
> *blowing its own squealing notes. And all the time the*

Master musician is waiting to play the most harmonious melody the world has ever heard.

As time passes, the little clarinet discovers metaphysics and begins to tell the Master Musician within what notes to play for it: "O Mighty Spirit, play the note for a new car for me, for money in the bank and a new job." At first this new way of playing brings results, but they are not lasting. Then the little clarinet seeks to make his demonstrations more "spiritual" and begins to listen for instructions from the Master within as to what notes to play: "Lord, give me the note for health and happiness and I will surely play it in your name." And again some fruit falls from the tree, but the taste is not satisfying. Finally the clarinet's consciousness evolves to the point where it declares, "I surrender to the great I AM THAT I AM. Master, play your notes through me!"

I chuckled when I read that. I see that I've been through the same process as that clarinet. Like the line "God make me an instrument of thy peace." What's then required for that to happen is that we actually ALLOW the Master Musician to play the instrument that is us. And our higher self has a higher perspective and access to all that is, so is really much better equipped to show a better path. And yet our mundane selves manifest that Divine Will into the world. The world can't hear the music of the Master Musician if we instruments are not here for It to play through.

BE THE HIGHER FREQUENCY PULLING OTHERS UP

Don't let others pull you down. You didn't gain this much ground just to slide back down. Now, the other may or may not be ready to be pulled up, but you're not serving yourself, them or the world by allowing them to suck you back down into a system that is on its way out.

In times of change, learners inherit the earth, while the learned find themselves beautifully equipped to deal with a world that no longer exists. - Eric Hoffer.

We're being given a grand opportunity to raise our frequency, both individually and collectively. Now, raising our frequency is not about "speeding up" per se. I watched a video of a sound healer.

He said that scientists used to think that a very low / slow brainwave frequency was only experienced when someone was sleeping or in a coma. They have now come to realize that this low frequency brainwave is also experienced while doing shamanic / healing work by both the practitioner and the person receiving the healing energy. It is through healing that we will raise our frequency. And the healing work slows us down. Slow brainwave, increased frequency.

This also reminds me of the line "stop and smell the roses." Rose essence is the highest frequency essence. If we stop to smell the roses, our frequency will go up. We've got to slow down to speed up.

In recent years, I have often felt like I am to anchor slow in a world of headless chickens, to set the example of taking it slow. In January of 2007, I had wanted to get a jump on getting into shape for the summer. I had been given many messages by Life to take things slow and my workout plans were obviously a little too ambitious for what Life had in mind for me.

I started doing some running and also got online to seek out racquetball partners. I went out one day to play racquetball for the first time in many years and thoroughly enjoyed myself and got a good workout. My next scheduled partner presented me with a different experience. He was late and it went downhill from there. I left there feeling very frustrated. It was midday and a beautiful day, so I went for a run. Due to my frustration and some other distractions, I ended up spraining my ankle big time, like I'd never done before. It was bad, but I didn't realize how bad till later that evening. At one point I'd wondered if it was broken. I could not put weight on it. I asked a friend to bring me some crutches. I was not working, so didn't need to go anywhere. After a week, I got out for groceries but that was about all the walking I could do and went home and collapsed. After another week, I could walk on it pretty good and I was getting cabin fever. It had snowed and there was still a bit of snow and ice on the ground, but I had to get out. I went for a walk. Due to my ankle and the ice I had to walk very slowly and cautiously.

At that point, I was given a vision that went like this – There was a wide, raging river to cross. The water was very chaotic, moving fast and splashing all around. There were stones placed at just the right distance apart and were just the right size and flat enough to make the river crossable by stepping on the stones. It was perfectly plain though that one false move would put you in a very cold, chaotic, wet place. The message from this was that these times we are in are quite passable, but we must move cautiously, deliberately and take things very slowly. Otherwise, we will get caught up in the swirling chaos.

This leads me to the definition of gluttony from the Enneagram of Personality theory, which speaks of nine personality types. Seven of the characteristic emotional passions or vices of the Enneatypes correspond with the traditional seven deadly sins with two additional "sins", deceit and fear, also included. Gluttony is defined: "not in the sense of eating too much but, rather, of sampling everything the world has to offer (breadth) and not taking the time for richer experience (depth)." So many people have gotten so caught up in the swirl of modern day life that they are literally surfing life and not having meaningful experiences. Life is meant to be savored. I don't care if we're taking about sipping on a nice organic, unfiltered and unpasteurized microbrew, as opposed to downing a case of better-living-through-chemistry "bad beer" swill, suffering through the taste and chemicals just to achieve that escapism buzz. If you're going to bother to indulge in such, at least pick the healthiest version out there and take your sweet time. It's ok if you taste it. No really.

Or we could be talking about prolonging the act of sex, rather than the wham-bam-thank-ya-ma'am "sport sex" that so many (too many) indulge in. If climax doesn't happen in a few minutes partners are asking each other what they're doing wrong or suggesting that they may not be sexually compatible. "Yes, honey, if your attention span is that short you're certainly not resonating with me. You in a rush? Ya got some better place to be? Be on your way then. Don't let the door hit ya in the ass on your way out." Sex is one of the most natural ways to connect Heaven to Earth and people want to fly through it. For goodness sakes, build that ecstatic energy slowly-but-surely 'cuz it's got some wonderful intentional applications that will help this world.

In spiritual quests, it's not about doing your duty by pew-sitting for one hour a week then forget about it the rest of the week. In Barbara Marciniak's book *Bringers of the Dawn*, the Pleiadians ask - How much time will one need to spend towards their lightwork here on Earth? All of it. You get the spark and you live and breathe it. You consider it in everything you do. In all cases, enjoy the journey, every step, every level.

The best energy to offer the world is your own joy, bliss, ecstasy and freedom, none of which come for free in this current world, even though they are a God-given right. All require that we face our wounds and demons and get down to the work of healing. But the payoff is HUGE. Not just for us, but for the world. Who would you rather be around, someone negative and whose life is full of drama and chaos or someone who is calm, centered and grounded, who has mastered the concept of compassionate non-attachment? Which one sends you a more positive vibe? If you can feel their vibes, you can bet everyone is feeling yours too. Which would you rather radiate?

Raise your own personal frequency and let that radiate out to the collective. It starts with self.

THE CALM IN THE CENTER OF THE STORM

So we come full circle, back to being self-centered. Would you like a world full of calm, peace and contentment? Who wouldn't? But is that what we are really creating "out there" when we can't seem to manage to create it "in here". When we only see chaos in our world and keep diving right into it, we end up in a very turbulent place, putting even more energy into something we claim we don't want.

I spent some time doing some martial arts. I learned that when attempting a kick or other maneuver, especially when standing on one foot, what helps you keep your balance is to breathe into your center - two inches below your belly button. The calmest part of a tornado or hurricane is in the eye, the center of the storm. And the calmest part of ourselves and our reality is our center. Martial arts is one demonstration of how this is played out physically, but it also applies mentally, emotionally and spiritually. Our breath is so very vital. And it's not just about keeping us alive, but to also truly BE living while alive. Any time you feel off center, in chaos, off balance, breathe into your center. You can have bombs dropping all around you and you will still find calm at your center. There is no better place to be centered but on self.

145

As I have emphasized throughout this book, start with self, return to self, maintain, love and respect self, heal thyself, know thyself. We won't find God and wisdom "out there" we'll find it "in here". We won't solve the world's problems while we're thrashing around in everyone else's drama, we'll find the calm in our center and radiate it out to a world that so desperately requires it.

BRING HEAVEN TO EARTH - RAISE EARTH TO HEAVEN

Jesus H. Christ!

I often use that exclamation because it opens up an opportunity to spread some light. Why do we say such things? Where does such come from? 'H' is a symbol of Jacob's ladder, the stairway to Heaven, ascension. At some level, we all know this. This is why such sayings exist in our language, even though many don't understand why they say it. So it is in all due respect for an ascended master (or at least an archetypal representation of that) that I use that exclamation. Abram of the Old Testament became Abraham, and Sara became Sarah. The 'H' added to their name symbolizes that both had achieved ascension. Both made the connection between Heaven and Earth while in physical form.

Kathianne Lewis from the Center for Spiritual Living once talked about Jesus having a "what am I doing here with these people" moment when his followers kept wanting to worship him. In so doing, they were totally missing the point of what he was all about. He did not want their worship. He was serving as an example of what could be achieved *by humans*. He told them that what they were witnessing with him was not about him, but what worked through him. He was allowing the Divine to work through him. And when he said "I am the way, the truth and the light," it was not from him, but God speaking *through* him. Jesus was having a human / earthly experience as surely as his disciples were. If he could do it, so could they. He was attempting to empower them to let them know that what worked through him could also work through them. As the line attributed to Jesus goes, "Have I not said ye are gods? You too shall do these and greater things." We all can be that conduit to connect Heaven or Infinite Consciousness to Earth. Acknowledge the power you really possess and utilize it.

146

We all will be Christed when we hear ourselves say
We are that which we pray

Lyrics from "Innocence Maintained" by Jewel

I think the word Christian is missing a bump. Instead of an 'n' on the end, it could stand to be an 'm', then it would read Christ I am.

And, in order to be that antenna connecting Heaven to Earth, it's critical that we be here, be now. I've known so many folks who are very spiritual. We all really ought to be, very naturally so, since that's who we are and where we're from. It's a natural connection. But many of those spiritual folk are walking about three feet off the ground - one foot in spirit, the other on a banana peel, always looking for the escape, just can't wait to get outta here. Oh, if I had a nickel for every time I heard some spiritual person say, "I'm not coming back here again" when they're really not here now. You came here to be here, so be here. You cannot help this world if you are constantly looking for a way out through escapism and avoidance. And spirituality is an altered state, just as surely as drugs can be, and it can be used as an escape, just as surely as drugs. On the flip side, some drugs, if consumed with the proper Intent can be used for enlightenment, as can spirituality, if it too is approached with the proper Intent.

Dr. Heather Anne Harder wrote a book called *Many Were Called, Few Were Chosen - The Story of Mother Earth and the Earth-Based Volunteers*. Heather points out that many advanced souls were called to volunteer to help Mother Earth heal and raise her frequency in these wondrous times that are presently upon us. We, as individuals and as a race, are being offered a choice now between extinction and evolution. "Many were chosen." Chosen by whom? Chosen of themselves. The lightworkers here now are here of their own accord. This "army" of spiritual warriors was not drafted, they volunteered. We volunteered. We have come here to this time and place to help Mother Earth. Even those of us who have been here, done this, bought the T-shirt so many times that we have literally graduated beyond Earth's "lessons" / experiences, we too still check in here to have a human / earthly experience in these times to help Mother Earth increase her frequency. We come here to be here. We share in these experiences with those less advanced / experienced souls so that we can better relate to them.

147

We heal our own wounds from past and present life times and we also unload some of Mother Earth's burden. The healing, clearing and releasing work done by lightworkers is increasing.

There is no doubt in my mind and heart that's what I personally am here for. Mother Earth was the first entity I "heard" in my head. Astrologically, I chose some very grounding energy to check into this realm with. I didn't want my mundane self to miss the fact that I am here for Mother Earth. The first step being to work on my own healing and growth, to take those human / earthly lessons and help others with similar experiences. Things most certainly are speeding up lately as we wind down to the bottom of this Involutionary spiral. Involve is the opposite of Evolve. When we "bottom out", we'll then start the spiral of Evolution back up again. The spiral down has gotten to be tighter as we get close to the bottom. The spiral will be tight again in the first part of going back up again. Wee! With this increased speed, there are literally times that my teachers are a half a step ahead of me and I am half a step ahead of anyone I can then teach. There are times when I have literally just learned something when Life puts someone else with the same lesson right in front of me.

It's said that the true master is the teacher-ever-student, knowing that even as the scales tip more towards teaching than learning, the learning never truly stops. If it does, then the growth also stops. I feel for those folks who already know everything, for they've nothing left to learn and that's got to be boring.

Jay Weidner was on the Mike Hagan radio show (www.mikehagan.com). He said he was giving away an alchemical secret. He spoke of the magnetic field around the Earth as being a toroid or donut-shaped (torus). What this means for us on the ground is that these magnetic lines of force are almost straight up and down. They run through us from head to toe, toe to head. This gives much power in being upright, being vertical. Some tribal people say that other animals are not as close to us in this regard as trees are. Yes, trees are the ultimate antennas. This vertical thing is why in tantric sex the partners sit upright. Their chakras and skeletal structures are maintained in a vertical position, allowing their resulting Kundalini energy to pulsate along the vertical lines of the magnetic field of the Earth. And if you cut horizontally into an apple, which is also toroidal in shape, you'll see the pattern of the seeds in a pentagram. It looks much like Leonardo da Vinci's *Vitruvian Man*. A man creating a pentagram as he stands with hands stretched to the heavens.

Set your intentions to be a clear channel between Heaven and Earth. Visualize yourself as a pillar of light connecting Earth to Heaven. Assume the Orans or 'Y' Prayer Posture, tap into your internal sun at the solar plexus chakra, breathe deep into your center (two inches below your belly button) and literally WILL Earth to connect to the Kingdom of Heaven. Utilize your ecstatic energy, no matter how you develop it, as a generator to manifest your intentions to help this world raise its frequency.

Are we there yet?

NOTHING NEW UNDER THE SUN

We've really nothing to learn and nothing to teach. We can only re-member and re-mind. Re-member – put the members back together: body, mind, spirit, emotions. Re-mind – put your mind back into it.

Have you heard all or part of what I've said here elsewhere? Of course you have. I've referenced and quoted a bunch of sources. Life is sending many to help us save ourselves from sin (ignorance). The message is coming from so many people and yet so many are yet to "hear" it. And so the next person then carries the torch to the next and we have the same wonderful message communicated in all diverse ways being repeated over and over until we reach a critical mass of enlightened folk. This message is coming into the world through many sources. It's being presented in all manner of ways so that all manner of people get the opportunity to "hear" it in a language they may understand. None of this is new. This is why many folks refer to such as ancient wisdom. It's been around longer than we as a race have been.

Fundamentals. Fun-duh-mentals. Yes, very basic. Wisdom IS very basic, very fundamental, very simple. And yet we all seem to need constant re-minders. It's no wonder, considering we've been conditioned so hard and so long in a dysfunctional, disempowering way, that we now need to condition ourselves in another direction. Through this, we could stand to make better choices daily about the environment we put ourselves into, the food we eat, the information we expose ourselves to, the company we keep, the thoughts we think, the emotions we emote. It will require we be patient with ourselves. There is no "quick fix". We wouldn't expect to condition ourselves to be a couch potato for years then suddenly get up off the couch and run a marathon and think that we won't suffer the consequences of doing so... if we live to tell about it. And yet if we set our Intent and stick to it, the changes can happen far quicker than we might first think. There are fast tracks. Then the snowball affect kicks in. Soon we will find ourselves in a very empowered state of being.

And yet there are still so many folks who still can't see through their conditioning. As far as sharing the ancient wisdom with each other, I see the conditioning show up on both sides. Many people have and are continuing to create ways to make a living out of sharing the light. Some get caught up in the money side of it and forget their beginnings and why they got into this in the first place. Just like with education, the medium has become the message - doesn't matter what's being sold, if the commerce mentality can just keep ya buying things, even spirituality, it's got ya. There's nothing wrong with making a living at these types of things. There's everything right with it. It's most certainly not any worse than any conventional means of earning a living. Where the issue seems to be is when people won't share not one little tidbit of wisdom unless they can charge for it. I've watched folks spend more time not giving an answer than what it would take to just give the answer. That doesn't make much sense at any level. How profitable is your time if it's spent dodging questions? Obviously some still do not understand the Law of Abundance and what you put out comes back to you... and it need not come from those you gave to. No need to be tit for tat when you're working with energy. The energy will find its way back to you.

I once read online a sermon by a Baptist minister. He spoke of a parable that Jesus had told. The way the parable goes is this – three men were given a sum of money that they could use for a specified period of time, then it must be returned. The first man invested his money into a business and worked moderately hard to create a profit. The second man also invested his portion of money into a business, worked even harder, made even more profit. The third man took his portion of money, buried it in the ground and went about living life the way he had. All were taken care of in life and when the time arrived for them all to return the money, all were able to do so.

This Baptist minister said that this parable often gets used by churches around tithing time to get people to tithe more. It's almost the attitude of buying your way into Heaven – give more and you'll get back more. Well, give more to what? To an enslaving economic system that just feeds on greed and the attitude of "more, more more?" They missed the real message in this parable, as they did not take into consideration the context this parable was told in, that being a time when the Roman Empire was attempting to enslave people to an economic system (sound familiar?). The first two men in the parable were swept up into the economic system and busted their butts to "grow" their money. The third man did not get sucked up into the enslavement of the economic system. He was the true hero of this story and yet in these modern times, those telling this parable are as sucked up into the economic system as the first two men in this story. They, perhaps unwittingly, have twisted this story around to promote the very thing that Jesus was warning of by telling it in the first place.

The flip side of this money thing is those folks who don't want to invest any time, money or effort into their own healing and growth. Anyone or anything that may be of help in that regard, well, that's just too much to pay for THAT. Never mind all they spend for all manner of addiction or poor food, or entertainment of the sort that is just keeping them down. Yep, the conditioning has been strong and will be tough to turn around. No doubt. But we certainly can become more self aware of our attitudes towards such.

There are many books being sold and seminars offered about this wisdom that will one day not only be taught to us at a young age, but we will be drenched in it, day in and day out, instead of being slathered in disempowering propaganda as we have been for millennia. We will grow up in an environment that couldn't imagine being anything but this fundamentally wise.

As you read my work and those I reference, you'll see we don't agree on all things but those areas that jive are very interesting indeed and it's worth paying attention to these things. We're drawing on the same body of evidence and yet shining light onto all

151

parts, all angles of it. Just like Towelie, perhaps it not about "either / or" but "and / both." Perhaps all these perspectives are true. And considering that flushes out the bigger picture. Seemingly contradictory angles can both be true at once. You know you're really getting to the truth of things when you see that. This helps us to get past this illusion of polarity / duality. This is not so much about conflict and opposites as it is about complements.

If we continue down the old path, it may very well mean the demise for the race called human that we come here and borrow earthly vehicles from. As far as experiences go at this level, there seems to be nothing new under a 3-dimensional sun. We've been here, done this, bought the T-shirt. All we can do now at that level is repeat the same experiences. Enough already!

Dr. Joseph Dispenza in *What the Bleep!? Down the Rabbit Hole*, says that our frontal lobes are what allows for our free will. When we don't actually exercise our free will, we create nothing new. "As long as we choose based on what we know, we'll always get what we know." There's the line, "If you always do what you've always done, you'll always get what you've always got." If you want something different, then do, be, think, feel something different. Connect into consciousness. Perceive that you are something else, something other than a prisoner in this illusion. We start with dreams and imagination. This creates on other levels, which is important whether we draw those dreams into this realm or not. Dream big.

Create something new by daring to step out of what you've always known and always done. This is some of what the symbol of the vesica pisces (piscis) represents. It's a circle intersecting another circle. The Master Card symbol is a vesica pisces. One circle represents our known experience, the other the unknown. The overlap between the circles marks the portal between those two realms. We can step into a new realm without having to totally leave the other. We can step into a new realm without loosing our "anchor," if you will. Being courageous enough to step out into the unknown is how we grow, how we create. It's time for something new.

OUR TOP PRIORITY

There is nothing more precious than the self. - Yogi Tea Bag Tab Wisdom

The subtitle of this book is "Top Priority - Self". The word origin of priority literally means former. The word origin of former is foremost. The word origin of foremost is first. Within those definitions there is no talk of "only" or "exclusive". Taking care of oneself does not mean NOT helping others. It just puts things in the proper order. Crawl before you walk, walk before you run. Can you imagine attempting to put most first graders into grad school? How well would that work? Oh, only about as well as putting the world's issues above and before your own.

It's tough to tap into the energy of joy, bliss, happiness, peace, compassion and love when we're so caught up in the busy-busy, so distracted by the material world, keeping one's nose to the grindstone, putting that nose into everyone else's busy-ness. Taking care of oneself first is NOT selfish. It is ultimately what ENABLES us to help others and the world.

The people who are creating the global control agenda to enslave and disempower humans want you to be as far away from yourself as you can be, whether it be through time or distance. Why? Because our greatest power is in being right here, right now. And they know that. They've known us better than we've known ourselves and that's why they could influence us to put energy into the very things that we don't want.

I've noticed that people want to help and will quickly sign that check to supposedly save the starving, poverty stricken person on the other side of the world, and yet will think the homeless person in their hometown, standing in front of them, is disgusting or lazy or a whole string of negative terms. When confronted with that homeless person, they will do everything they can to not connect with their fellow human that stands before them. Perhaps if the person on the other side of the world they wrote the check for were standing in front of them, they'd think they were disgusting and avoid them also. The wounded part of people just wants it all to magically disappear, as if hearing about it happening "over there" is bad, but seeing it right before their very eyes just doesn't make people want to put a quarter in that homeless person's hand, or offer

153

them a free but priceless hug. It's as if people are getting all caught up in the global "out there" drama and yet still don't want any of it to come home with them.

And facing one's *own* wounds and demons is WAY too close to home. As if those wounds and demons will just go away if ignored long enough. Well, that's a nice fantasy, but I've yet to see anyone's problems go away by ignoring them. The people in front of you are closer to you than those folks on the other side of the world and you are as close to you as you can get. Your issues aren't going anywhere - no matter where you go, there you are.

People have been conditioned to take all the world's drama personally and yet don't tend to their own needs and don't personally want to radiate love to those people who stand right in front of them. People have been conditioned to fret over a future that may never happen. My father used to say, "Don't cry. It might never happen." And people have been conditioned to stew on the past. The past is called the past for a reason. It's done with. Sure, one doesn't want to wipe their memories clean, as the lessons learned go with those memories, so it doesn't serve us to throw out the baby with the bath water, but the emotional charge from the past can be released so we can now respond to life rather than that re-act (act over again). Time-wise, our greatest power comes from being present. Place-wise, our greatest power comes from being here.

You athletic types can probably relate to this. Have you ever played softball or baseball? Have you noticed that there are those players who think that their teammate is incapable of playing their position? Then the first player attempts to play both their own and their teammate's position. That sure causes a lot of problems. They get in the way of their teammate and leave a big hole where their own position is. Both positions basically go uncovered. Wouldn't it just be easier to play our own positions / roles and let others play theirs? If you'd like to guide someone in playing their role better, have at it, but don't think you can play their position for them, live their life for them, have their experiences for them. It's not your place.

If you hired someone to clean up your backyard and you got a chance to see their own yard first, who would you hire, the one who had a well groomed yard or the one who had something just shy of a junkyard in their back yard? Ah, the cobbler's children have no shoes. How old is that saying? Have we learned anything from the wisdom therein? Many folks who do yard maintenance probably do have messy yards. Hasn't that been the way of this world?! Do you like the state this world is presently in? See any room for improvement? Rather than biting off more than you can chew, you know, "over there", don't you think that maybe, just maybe, cleaning up your own little dirt piles would make more of a difference?

Not much of anything is being addressed, solved, re-paired when our focus is "out there". If we are not focused on ourselves, then who is? Should we just exchange checks back and forth? We can send a check to Africa and someone there can send one back to our neighbor? We can adopt a Chinese child. Are there Chinese citizens, in turn, who are adopting the parentless children in America?

As you expand out from yourself, then doing small things for others is still expressing self-love. And as the illusion of separation comes apart, we'll know anything we do for others we do for ourselves. "I am *that*." There are so many opportunities to do little things for others, something that takes little effort on our part and yet means so much for the receiver... and others. Wayne Dyer was on the Ellen show talking about kindness. He spoke of the natural "feel good" chemical serotonin. He said a study was done measuring serotonin levels in people receiving acts of kindness. Yes, their serotonin levels went up. But so did the serotonin levels of those offering the kindness. Most profound though was that those witnessing those acts of kindness also had their serotonin levels raised to the same level as those giving and receiving kindness. It's energetically contagious. It helps self, others and the world.

In my own personal life, I have found the more I tap into my higher self, the less "work" I'm really doing. As I follow the guidance from my higher self, I still need to do my part on a mundane level in manifesting, but I find I make less wasted motion. Every move counts. All my efforts go towards my higher purpose and are not spent on distractions, wheel spinning or tail chasing. In essence, my life becomes simpler and easier and yet all my needs are satisfied. The "work" I do doesn't feel like work anymore when it's what's in line with my higher purpose. It's the kind of stuff I like to do. So, I'm basically not working, not struggling, not aching... just living. I'm having it all and not knocking myself out to have it.

Since I have less to do and more time, always ahead of the game, I am now more available to people in the moment. I've, at times, called myself a Spiritual Minuteman because I have tended to my own needs first, followed my inner guidance, which takes less effort to provide the same or greater results, which then creates a situation where I have more to give to others. Now when I say, "give", for the most part I'm not talking about giving of material goods or money, but giving of myself. This is what most people want, need and could use the most – someone who will acknowledge them and simply say hi, someone just spending some time with them, someone who will lend an ear, someone who, at the drop of a hat can help them out with something, someone who is not so hurried and caught up in the busyness of life that they have no time for them... someone who has the time and energy to actually do random acts of kindness.

Jean Shinoda Bolen who promotes, amongst other things, the necessary balance that feminine energy brings, says she uses three criteria to determine if she gets involved with something - is it meaningful, fun and motivated by love? Jean says that even outrage energy can still be motivated by love for something or someone. As you may be able to tell by this point, my passion is to share information with people in hopes of empowering them. And you can bet that fits all three of Jean's criteria for me. What works for you? Make sure you have the energy to do it, and the proper quality of energy that comes from taking care of yourself first.

I can't stress "maintenance" enough. Maintain your health, at all levels. As I'd mentioned earlier, Michael Tsarion (www.michaeltsarion.com) talks about hygiene. We are so concerned with hygiene. We're always bathing, washing our clothes, cleaning the house, washing the car. We often forget about our emotional, psychological and spiritual hygiene. It no more serves us to let our emotional, psychological garbage pile up than it does to let our home garbage waste pile up. Take out the garbage regularly.

Now, if we fill our own cups first, and maintain our own cups, that is what allows us to be of use to anyone else. We have the energy to do so and we have the proper *quality* of energy to influence others in an empowering way by sheer example or merely with our presence. The order of priorities is to start with self. When self is maintained and overflowing, then deal with the people who are right in front of you, then perhaps you can eventually help on a more global level.

So, you see, I'm not telling you not to help others or even those on the other side of the world. What we are doing here on this planet in these times goes beyond this planet even. It is making an impact across the multi-verse. What I am telling you is, if you make yourself your top priority, this will better enable you, prepare you, equip you to help the world if you so choose and you can lead by example, and your energy radiates out ahead of you. If you can take care of yourself, what's in front of you and help the global situation, then have at it. That's what I'm doing right here, right now by writing this book. You can bet I am only working on this when the time is right, when my energy is right. This creative process is a joy, not a chore by any means, and I keep it that way by not forcing it, by self-nurturing when need be.

I also cannot emphasize enough that the energetic level is the most subtle and yet the most significant and powerful. There are times I'll stay away from people to help those very people that I'm staying away from. I'll stay out of crowds so as not to take on their "negative" energy, to keep my energy "pure," so as to radiate that out on the energetic levels. At other times, intermingling my energy with theirs is what's called for. And if my energy is "down," then how much am I serving the world by insisting on putting my energy out to others, delivering my bad mood?

Go ahead and care about those "out there" and on the other side of the world. Send them your love and joy. Work on the energetic level. Start with self. Send yourself that love and joy first. It's the inner work that will change the outer world, which is just a reflection, a manifestation of our inner realms.

> *"Peace in the world must begin first within the heart and purpose and mind of the individual...[for] as individuals change themselves and their interactions with one another, eventually the world cannot help but follow." –* Edgar Cayce

Be patient with yourself and with the process. We don't sink to the bottom overnight and we won't rise again overnight either. Don't get stuck in "either / or." If you're not ready to make the best choice, at least make the better choice. Crawl before you walk, walk before you run, but for goodness sakes, move onward and upward.

Work on you, work for you, work with you. Self-love, self-respect, self-nurturing, self-compassion, self-centeredness.

Start with self.

We can break the cycle - We can break the chain
We can start all over - In the new beginning
We can learn, we can teach
We can share the myths the dream the prayer
The notion that we can do better
Change our lives and paths
Create a new world and

Start all over...

Lyrics from "New Beginning" by Tracy Chapman

Afterward

I started this book around June of 2007. In the first six months, the words and inspirations just flowed out of me. The first half of the book was a total breeze. The second half's topics I had down, sometimes in expanded paragraphs, sometimes only in very sketchy notes, but it was mostly all there. Then 2008 came. I don't know if you also felt 2008 was pivotal, but I certainly did. And as "pivotal" and "turning points" imply, you often hit bottom before changing directions.

My lifelong career certainly seemed to be reaching a dead end. Even if I found jobs where the work was right up my alley, that I was very good at and also thoroughly enjoyed, then management would throw a wrench in the works, even if that ultimately meant shooting themselves in the foot. It reminded me of the message of the movie Mindwalk – we have to change our perspectives at a very fundamental level. Anything less is just a band-aid. And the politics in my career was just evidence of that need for fundamental change across the board in this world, not just in that industry. Towards the end of 2008, the message came to me of these times not being about "fixing" anyone or anything, but just another re-minder of "creating" the change. I knew that even being in that environment of my old career with the outdated mentality of so many I worked with was not serving me, them or the world. I had to create an environment for myself that allowed me to truly live the change, to truly be the example and not just beating against the old system.

In the early part of 2009 I continued working on this book and, as I went through my notes, I very much felt like my life, in general, was at the point of no return. I was beyond fed up with "the old system," as I call it. It reminds me of something from an Orson Scott Card sci-fi novel – in the future a planet had been colonized by Samoan people who were easy going and very patient, but when pushed too much they would eventually reach the point of "Enough Already!" I find that "fed up" energy closely precedes great change. As we make the shift in these interesting times we are in, we are moving into "uncharted territory" and sometimes may have a tough time expressing what it is we really want because we're not totally sure of the possibilities and just how quickly those possibilities can manifest. Sometimes how Life guides us is by showing us what we don't want. By defining and refining exactly what it is we no longer want to witness or experience, we can better define and refine exactly what we do want to create.

I was most certainly ready for something new and knew that I had to be part of that change. I could not just spectate from the sidelines or continue to find little opportunities in my day to day to present a more empowering perspective to my fellow human. I knew the pressure of a crumbling "old system" would provide the catalyst for change in a much bigger way that would affect the masses. Others would soon come to realize that, yes, indeed, something had to give, shift was becoming more and more inevitable.

Through this turning point, I myself could have used some guidance. Interestingly enough, I found that guidance in my own words that I'd already written as I worked through this book. The book provided its own encouragement for me to continue down a new path. I say this because you too have your own inner guidance. Your own words are filled with wisdom. I intend that this book assist you in finding the courage and faith to trust in yourself.

Thank you all for the work you do in this world.

And Mommy Earth thanks you also and sends you her love.

Awake & Aware -Top Priority: Self

BIBLIOGRAPHY

BOOKS

The Holographic Universe by Michael Talbot
I Need Your Love: Is That True? by Byron Katie
Adam & Evil, The God Who Hates Sex, Women & Human Bodies by The Heyeokah Guru
Heal Your Body by Louise Hay
The Healing Sun Code by William Henry
Essential Reiki by Diane Stein
Wheels of Life: A User's Guide to the Chakra System by Anodea Judith
The Magdalen Manuscript, The Alchemies of Horus & The Sex Magic of Isis by Tom Kenyon and Judi Sion
The Alphabet Versus the Goddess by Leonard Schlain
Blink by Malcolm Gladwell
Magdalene's Lost Legacy by Margaret Starbird
Bringers of the Dawn by Barbara Marciniak
Natural Cures "They" Don't Want You to Know About by Kevin Trudeau
Receiving Prosperity by Louise Hay
Conversations With God by Neale Donald Walsch
Heal Your Wounds and Find Your True Self by Lise Bourbeau
Face Reading in Chinese Medicine by Lillian Bridges
The Wisdom of Your Face by Jean Haner
Relationships: Gifts of the Spirit by Julie Hutslar.
Secret Life of Plants by Peter Tompkins and Christopher Bird
Biology of Belief by Bruce Lipton
The Frontal Lobes Supercharge by Neil Slade
Traveling the Interstate of Consciousness: A Driver's Instruction Manual by Patricia Leva
Infinite Love is All There Is, Everything Else is Illusion by David Icke
The Language of the Birds by William Henry
The Angels Within Us by John Randolph Price
Many Were Called, Few Were Chosen by Heather Anne Harder

ARTICLES

Holographic Universe article www.crystalinks.com/holographic.html
Against School article by John Taylor Gatto -
www.spinninglobe.net/againstschool.htm
What are Indigo and Crystal Children and Adults -
www.starchild.co.za/what.html
Lucifer – where did the word come from and what is its true
meaning - www.lds-mormon.com/lucifer.shtml
Moses and Those 'Horns' by Eloise Hart -
www.theosociety.org/pasadena/sunrise/23-73-4/mi-elo.htm
Some Light on Lucifer by Ina Beldris - www.theosophy-
nw.org/theosnw/world/christ/xt-ibel2.htm
The Battle of Darkness & Light by Mary Sparrowdancer -
www.rense.com/general45/bll.htm
Eating dirt can be good for you – just ask babies by Jane E. Brody –
(use search engine)

MOVIES

Zeitgeist the movie zeitgeistmovie.com/
Making a Killing – The Untold Story of Psychotropic Drugging
Mindwalk (check with specialty video stores)
What the Bleep!? Down the Rabbit Hole www.whatthebleep.com
Freedom to Fascism by Aaron Russo
Sicko by Michael Moore

VIDEOS

Revelations of a Mother Goddess, with Arizona Wilder by David Icke
Starwalkers and the Dimension of the Blessed by William Henry
Reptilian Agenda, video interview with Credo Mutwa by David Icke
Receiving Prosperity, video by Louise Hay
Earth Under Fire, video based on the work of Paul LaViolette
Secrets of Alchemy, video by Jay Weidner
Quantum Astrology: Science, Spirit and Our Place in the Cycle of
History, video by Rick Levine
Loose Change 2nd Edition – documenting the information about
9/11 hidden from the public

WEBSITES

Joanie Vogel - www.energysinger.com/forecast.html
Michael Tsarion - www.michaeltsarion.com
William Henry - www.williamhenry.net
David Icke – www.davidicke.com
Margaret Starbird - www.margaretstarbird.net
Richard C. Hoagland - www.enterprisemission.com
Don Miguel Ruiz & Don Jose Luis Ruiz - www.miguelruiz.com
Dr. Lorraine Day - www.drday.com
Dogtor J, John B. Symes, D.V.M. - www.dogtorj.net/index.html
Jean Haner - www.wisdomofyourface.com
Fereydoon Batmanghelidj M.D. - www.watercure.com
Elaine Smitha - www.elainesmitha.com
Dr. Mercola - www.mercola.com
Bruce Lipton, PhD - www.brucelipton.com
Joyce Riley - www.gulfwarvets.com
Dr. Leonard Horowitz - www.tetrahedron.org
Gary Craig, Emotional Freedom Technique - www.emofree.com
Gregg Braden - www.greggbraden.com
Tom Bearden - www.cheniere.org
Dr. Lee Pulos - www.drpulos.com
Walter Cruttenden - www.binaryresearchinstitute.org
John Major Jenkins - alignment2012.com
Paul LaViolette - www.etheric.com
Seattle Metaphysical Library - www.seattlemetaphysicallibrary.org
Sean David Morton - www.delphiassociates.org
Jay Weidner - www.jayweidner.com
Doreen Virtue - www.angeltherapy.com
Eckhart Tolle - www.eckharttolle.com
Wayne Dyer - www.drwaynedyer.com
Jean Shinoda Bolen - www.jeanshinodabolen.com

RADIO SHOWS AND VIDEO INTERVIEWS

Conscious Media Network - www.consciousmedianetwork.com
Mike Hagan's Radio Orbit - www.mikehagan.com
Coast to Coast AM - www.coasttocoastam.com
News for the Soul - www.newsforthesoul.com

Made in the USA
Lexington, KY
18 April 2015